Anunnaki Gods or Almighty God

BOOK 2

Author:
Our True History

Cover design:
Mark Thomas

© MMXXV Ebens Publishing
World Copyright 2025 Our True History /
Ebens Publishing. All rights reserved.

ISBN: 9798272184436

Chapters

Chapter	Title	Page
1	Who Jehovah was	7
2	Enki – Roman / Greek	18
3	Enlil – Roman / Greek	28
4	Inanna – Roman / Greek	34
5	Dragons	39
6	Anunnaki created us twice	47
7	Mark of the beast	67
8	Jesus's father	81
9	Why Jesus was born	93
10	Demons	104
11	Ark of the Covenant	110
12	Cherubim	119
13	Heaven	124
14	Hell	132
15	Spirit	140
16	Other researchers	202
17	Lesser Gods / Igigi	209
18	Important tablets	214
19	Almighty God	236

Preface

Welcome to the second instalment of Almighty God, or Anunnaki Gods, a continuation of the groundbreaking journey begun in Book 1.

In the first volume, I introduced readers to the compelling evidence that the Anunnaki, an advanced extraterrestrial race, would have been the *""Gods"1"* referenced in ancient texts, including the Bible.

By meticulously analysing ancient Sumerian tablets, biblical translations like Young's Literal Translation, and overlooked historical records, I challenged conventional narratives about humanity's origins, the nature of divinity, and the influence of these beings on our planet.
In this second book, I dive deeper into the mysteries surrounding the Anunnaki, their legacy, and their potential ongoing influence on Earth.

This volume expands on the connections between ancient history and modern institutions, further unravelling the threads of our true past. My goal remains the same: to present evidence with fairness, clarity, and an unwavering commitment to truth, allowing you to decide for yourself whether the Anunnaki were the Gods of our ancestors or if an Almighty God stands alone.

OUR TRUE HISTORY

For those eager to explore more, my website, www.ourtruehistory.co.uk, is a treasure trove of resources that complement and expand upon the ideas in both books.

Here, you'll find exclusive documentaries, in-depth videos, and detailed analyses covering topics like the Anunnaki, their home planet Nibiru, ancient civilizations, and unexplained phenomena such as Bigfoot, crystal skulls, Stonehenge, Easter Island, and even time travel and so much more.

Each piece is backed by years of research, drawing from ancient texts, archaeological findings, and modern scientific insights.
The website also hosts my viral TikTok videos, where I debunk misinformation and share never-before-seen evidence that has captivated nearly 300,000 followers with millions of views. Whether you're new to these subjects or a seasoned researcher, www.ourtruehistory.co.uk is your gateway to uncovering the hidden truths of our past.

This book builds on that foundation, offering fresh evidence and bold conclusions that challenge what we've been told about our history, our Gods, and our place in the cosmos. Prepare to question everything you thought you knew.

If Book 1 opened your eyes to the possibility that the Anunnaki shaped humanity's story, Book 2 will take you further into the shadows of history, revealing how their influence may still resonate today.

Visit www.ourtruehistory.co.uk to join the growing community of truth-seekers and dive into the documentaries that bring these discoveries to life. Thank you for continuing this journey with me.
There are other books I would highly recommend:

Area 51, Stonehenge, Crystal Skulls, Poltergeist and Our Untold History.

Atlantis, Mermaids, Pixies, Giants, and Our Untold History.

Black Ops, Aliens, Spirits, Bigfoot and Our Untold History.

Available on Amazon, Kindle, Audible, and Spotify audiobooks, these books weave together evidence from ancient civilizations, unexplained phenomena, and modern mysteries to reveal a unified story of humanity's past.

Together, they form a tapestry of knowledge that questions mainstream history and invites readers to explore the extraordinary.

Chapter 1

Who Jehovah Really Was!

In the Bible, the name Jehovah is used in various ways depending on the translation. Its frequency depends on how translators render the Tetragrammaton (YHWH), the four Hebrew letters representing the name of God.

King James Version (KJV):
The name Jehovah appears four times in the Old Testament:
- Exodus 6:3
- Psalm 83:18
- Isaiah 12:2
- Isaiah 26:4

New World Translation (NWT):
This translation, used by Jehovah's Witnesses, restores the name Jehovah over 7,000 times wherever the Tetragrammaton (YHWH) appears in the Hebrew Scriptures.

Modern Translations:
Many modern Bibles, such as the New International Version (NIV) or English Standard Version (ESV), do not use *"Jehovah."* Instead, they substitute it with *"LORD"* (in all caps) to reflect the Jewish tradition of reading YHWH as Adonai (Lord) or Elohim (God).
The use of Jehovah depends on whether the translation aims to include the divine name directly or follow the tradition of substituting it with *"LORD."* Notably, even Young's Literal Translation includes the name Jehovah.

The name Jehovah originates from the Hebrew יהוה (YHWH), known as the Tetragrammaton. In Greek, the Tetragrammaton lacks a direct equivalent because ancient Greek cannot precisely represent it. In the Septuagint (the Greek translation of the Hebrew Scriptures), YHWH is often replaced with the Greek word Κύριος (Kyrios), meaning *"Lord."*

Other renderings or interpretations of YHWH/Jehovah based on linguistic and theological perspectives include:
1. Kyrios (Κύριος)
   Meaning: *"Lord"* or *"Master."*
   The most common substitution in the Septuagint and used in the New Testament when quoting Hebrew Scriptures.
2. Theos (Θεός)
   Meaning: *"God."*
   Used in Greek Scriptures to refer to God in a general sense, though not a direct translation of YHWH.
3. Iao (Ιαω)
   A transliteration of YHWH in some ancient Greek sources, including early manuscripts and magical texts, to preserve its phonetics.
4. Adonai
   The Hebrew word for *"Lord,"* spoken aloud by Jewish readers in place of YHWH out of reverence.
   In the Septuagint, Adonai became Kyrios.
5. Ehyeh (Ἐγώ Εἰμί)
   Meaning: *"I AM."*
   Derived from Exodus 3:14, where God identifies Himself as *"I AM THAT I AM"* (Hebrew: Ehyeh Asher Ehyeh).

In Greek, rendered as Ego Eimi, used in the New Testament, particularly by Jesus, to signify divinity (e.g., John 8:58).

To understand the meaning directly, the possible translations are:
- Kyrios (Κύριος): *"Lord"* or *"Master."*
- Theos (Θεός): *"God."*
- Iao (Ιαω): YHWH.
- Adonai: *"Lord."*
- Ehyeh (Ἐγώ Εἰμί): *"I AM."*

Focusing on the first, *"Lord"* or *"Master,"* the Bible uses *"lord"* for various figures. Mainstream sources state:
"The Bible mentions many lords, but it emphasises that there is only one true Lord, YHWH (Jehovah), or, in the New Testament, Jesus Christ. Other 'lords' refer to human authority figures or false Gods, which are not on the same level as the true divine Lord."

Of course, it does not say *"False Gods"* anywhere in the Bible, or does it?
Yes, Deuteronomy 32:17 is from the New International Version (NIV) of the Bible:
"They sacrificed to false Gods, which are not God, Gods they had not known, Gods that recently appeared, Gods your ancestors did not fear."

So, it is solved: there was really only one God (even though there were more). Not so fast!

Let us look at the literal version and not the NIV, which was first published in 1973. Seriously, who thinks that people in 1973 could change the wording to fit their agenda?

I say that because when you look here at Young's Literal Version, you will see there is a huge difference.

"17 They sacrifice to demons, no God! Gods they have not known, new ones, from the vicinity they came. Not feared them have your fathers!"

Sorry, but in that version, I cannot see false Gods. Basically, without going through the whole Bible and pointing out the errors, it simply tells us there are many Gods.

However, I believe this interpretation is flawed, as it assumes a single divine entity, whereas I have argued in other chapters that the Bible references multiple Gods. Specifically, I have shown that Yahweh was Marduk, the son of Enki. See my chapter, Who Yahweh Really Was, for details.

Why Mainstream Scholars Equate Jehovah to Yahweh

The name YHWH appears over 6,800 times in the Hebrew Scriptures. Since ancient Hebrew was written without vowels, the pronunciation of YHWH is uncertain. Scholars reconstruct *"Yahweh"* as the likely pronunciation based on linguistic studies. The name Jehovah emerged later, during the Middle Ages, by combining:
- The consonants of YHWH.
- The vowel points from Adonai (*"Lord"*), used in Jewish tradition to avoid pronouncing YHWH directly.

This assumes a single *"Lord,"* but I argue this is incorrect. In early Jewish tradition, out of reverence, Jews avoided saying YHWH aloud, substituting it with Adonai or Elohim. When the Masoretes (Jewish scribes, 6th–10th centuries CE) added vowel points to the Hebrew text, they inserted the vowels of Adonai into YHWH, resulting in the hybrid form that became Jehovah.

Biblical Evidence

In Genesis 2:7, *"the LORD God"* (Hebrew: YHWH Elohim) creates Adam from dust and breathes life into him.
In Genesis 2:16–17 (KJV):
"And the LORD God commanded the man, saying, Of every tree of the garden thou mayest freely eat: But of the tree of the knowledge of good and evil, thou shalt not eat of it..."

In Genesis 3:8, after Adam and Eve sin, they hear *"the voice of the LORD God"* walking in the garden and hide. In Young's Literal Translation, this becomes:
"And Jehovah God layeth a charge on the man, saying, 'Of every tree of the garden eating thou dost eat;'"

Notably, it uses *"Jehovah,"* not *"Yahweh."* Young's Literal Translation is one of the closest to the original Hebrew, yet I believe there is another way to interpret the Bible.

We know Enki created Homo sapiens, and Adapa and Titi were Adam and Eve, with Enki as their father. But was Enki called *"Lord God"* or *"Master"*?

Sumerian Texts

In tablets predating the Bible, such as Enki and Ninmah (c.1.1.2):
"Enki ... brought joy to their heart. He set a feast for his mother Namma and for Ninmah. ... An, Enlil, and Lord Nudimmud roasted holy kids. All the senior Gods praised him: 'O Lord of wide understanding, who is as wise as you? Enki, the great Lord, who can equal your actions? Like a corporeal father, you are the one who has the me of deciding destinies. In fact, you are the me.'"

This passage shows *"Lord"* applied to multiple figures, but Enki is called the *"great Lord."* Similarly, in Inana and Enki (c.1.3.1):
After Enki had spoken thus to him, Isimud the minister followed his master's instructions closely.

Many Anunnaki were called *"master,"* as each royal Anunnaki had workers who addressed them as such.

Anunnaki Lords
In Sumerian, Akkadian, Babylonian, and Assyrian texts, *"Lord"* (Sumerian: EN, meaning Lord or master) was reserved for deities with significant authority. Below are Anunnaki figures referred to as *"Lords"* and their domains:

- **Enki (Ea)** – *"The Great Lord of the Earth"*
Also called *"Lord of the Abzu"* (freshwater deep). Associated with wisdom, magic, creation, and water.
- **Enlil** – *"Lord of the Air"*
Supreme leader of the Anunnaki in many accounts, often called *"The Lord."*
- **Nannar** (Sin) – *"The Lord of Wisdom and the Moon"*
Son of Enlil, worshipped as the moon God.
- **Utu** (Shamash) – *"Lord of Justice"*
Sun God, enforcer of divine laws.
- **Ninurta** – *"Lord of War and Farming"*
Son of Enlil, called *"The Mighty Lord"* in some texts.
- **Marduk** – *"Lord of the Gods of Heaven and Earth"*
Elevated to supreme status in Babylon, titled Bel (*"Lord"*) in Akkadian.
- **Nergal** – *"Lord of the Underworld"*
God of war, plague, and the dead, partnered with **Ereshkigal.**
- **Dumuzi (Tammuz)** – *"Lord Shepherd"*

God of fertility and vegetation, called a *"Lord of the Land."*

Female Anunnaki (Lady Titles):
While *"Lord"* was male-gendered, female Anunnaki were called *"Lady"* (NIN in Sumerian), carrying equal divine authority:
- **Inanna (Ishtar)** – *"Lady of Heaven"*
Also *"The Great Lady"* or *"Mistress of the Gods,"* Goddess of love, war, and fertility.
- **Ereshkigal** – *"Lady of the Great Earth"* (Underworld)
Ruler of the underworld with absolute authority.
- **Ninhursag (Ki, Mama)** – *"Lady of the Mountain"*
Mother Goddess and healer, also *"Lady Birth-Giver"* or *"Mother of All Gods."*
- **Ninsun** – *"Lady of the Wild Cows"*
Mother of Gilgamesh, revered as a wise divine queen.
- **Ninlil** – *"Lady of the Wind"*
Wife of Enlil, with dominion over fate and wind.

Why Enki Could Be Jehovah?

Mainstream sources equate Jehovah with Yahweh, but I propose Jehovah was Enki. The earliest non-biblical mention of YHWH is from the 13th century BCE at the Temple of Soleb in Nubia, Egypt, where Pharaoh Amenhotep III lists *"the land of the Shasu of YHW,"* referring to nomads worshipping a deity named YHW (likely YHWH).
This aligns with Yahweh as Marduk, also known as Ra, the sun God, explaining the Egyptian connection.

In Genesis 2:4, *"the LORD God"* (Hebrew: YHWH Elohim) appears:

"These are the generations of the heavens and of the earth when they were created, in the day that the LORD God made the earth and the heavens."

An alternative translation based on ancient meanings could be:
"These are the records of the skies and the land when they were engineered, in the period when the Great Lord of the Powerful Ones fashioned the land and the skies."

Alternative Translations:
- Generations: Records, histories, accounts (tôlĕdôṯ can mean lineage or story of origins).
- Heavens: Skies, firmament, realms above (Hebrew shamayim; Sumerian An).
- Earth: Land, terrain, ground (Hebrew erets; Sumerian Ki).
- Created: Engineered, structured, assembled (Hebrew bara implies shaping or forming).
- Made: Fashioned, formed, constructed (Hebrew asah means to accomplish or fabricate).

In Exodus 3:13–15, YHWH reveals His name to Moses:
"God said to Moses, 'I AM WHO I AM.' And he said, 'Say this to the people of Israel: I AM has sent me to you.' ... This is my name forever, and thus I am to be remembered throughout all generations."

The phrase *"I AM WHO I AM"* (Ehyeh Asher Ehyeh) links to the Tetragrammaton, suggesting YHWH derives from the Hebrew root *"to be"* (h-y-h), emphasising God as eternal and self-existent. However, the phrase YHWH Elohim (*"the LORD God"*) indicates a specific divine entity, not necessarily an almighty universal God. I argue the *"God of Israel"* refers to Marduk, Enki's son, not a universal deity.

Evidence from Artifacts

The Mesha Stele (9th century BCE) mentions YHWH as the God of Israel, but this supports my view that the *"God of Israel"* is Marduk, not a universal God. At the British Museum (artefact 47406), a text suggests Babylonian scholars experimented with monotheism, equating major Gods to aspects of Marduk:

"In this text, the writer suggests that the major Babylonian Gods are merely aspects of the supreme God Marduk. In the left-hand column are the names of fourteen major Gods, and Marduk's name is repeated in the right-hand column on every line."

Jehovah appears 1,300 to 2,700 years after the earliest mentions of Yahweh. Raymundus Martini, a Catholic monk, was among the first to use the hybrid form Jehovah, combining YHWH's consonants with Adonai's vowels to avoid pronouncing the divine name.

Avoiding YHWH's Pronunciation.

Mainstream sources claim Jews avoided pronouncing YHWH to prevent misuse, citing:
- Exodus 20:7 (The Ten Commandments):
"You shall not take the name of the LORD (YHWH) your God in vain..."
I interpret this as *"don't speak ill of me,"* not *"never say my name."*
- Leviticus 24:16:
"Whoever blasphemes the name of the LORD (YHWH) shall surely be put to death."
Again, this suggests *"don't badmouth me,"* not *"avoid my name entirely."*

- Psalm 8:1:
"O LORD, our Lord, how majestic is your name in all the earth!"
Here, the name is celebrated, not forbidden.

By the Second Temple period (ca. 6th century BCE–70 CE), Jews substituted Adonai for YHWH when reading Scriptures aloud. The Masoretes (6th–10th centuries CE) added Adonai's vowel points to YHWH, resulting in Yehovah, later misunderstood as Jehovah.

The Talmud (Kiddushin 71a) notes the divine name was only spoken by the High Priest on Yom Kippur. Josephus (Antiquities of the Jews, Book 2, Chapter 12) confirms the name was ineffable for ordinary people. The Septuagint (3rd–2nd century BCE) uses Kyrios for YHWH, reflecting this practice.

However, there is no definitive evidence that Jehovah was created to avoid saying Yahweh, as Yahweh continued to be discussed after Jehovah's introduction. This weakens the mainstream argument.
I propose Jehovah was Enki, not Marduk (Yahweh). When Marduk became the main leader, replacing Enlil (then called El), the name Yahweh was assigned to him.

In Young's Literal Translation, *"Jehovah"* appears only in the Old Testament, while Jesus appears in the New Testament. Jehovah's stories involve:
- Creation (Genesis 2:4).
- Covenant with Abraham (Genesis 15).
- Deliverance of Israel from Egypt (Exodus 3:14–15).
- Giving the Ten Commandments (Exodus 20).

These align with Enki's attributes. In Genesis 15 (YLT):
Genesis 15:1:
"After these things hath the word of Jehovah been unto Abram in a vision, saying, 'Fear not, Abram, I [am] a shield to thee, thy reward [is] exceeding great.'"

Genesis 15:7:
"And He saith unto him, 'I [am] Jehovah who brought thee out from Ur of the Chaldees, to give to thee this land to possess it.'"

Ur, a major Sumerian city in modern southern Iraq, was home to the Great Ziggurat dedicated to Nanna (Sin), the moon God and son of Enlil. Genesis 15:18 (YLT) states:
"In that day hath Jehovah made with Abram a covenant, saying, 'To thy seed I have given this land, from the river of Egypt unto the great river, the river Euphrates...'"

Only Enki or Enlil had the authority to grant such land. Since Enki was Ptah in Egypt and associated with creation (*"to thy seed"*), Enki is the likely candidate for Jehovah.

Chapter 2
Enki - Which Greek and Roman God Was He?

Enki, known as Ea in Akkadian tablets, is a central figure in the Sumerian pantheon, revered across Mesopotamia. He was the God of wisdom, water, creation, fertility, and mischief. Enki was associated with the Abzu (Africa), and he was more commonly known as the God of water.
As a prince alongside his brother Enlil, he played a vital role in Sumerian cosmology.

Enki governed water sources, linking him to fertility and life-giving forces essential for agriculture in the Sumerian world.

Enki was the God of wisdom, intelligence, and magic, known for his knowledge of arts, sciences, and civilisation. He was invoked for guidance and protection in matters requiring cleverness.

In the Atrahasis flood tablet, Enki warned Noah (Atrahasis) of a great flood planned by the Gods to destroy humanity, instructing him to build a boat to save himself and the animals.

Enki's cunning and wisdom enabled him to resolve conflicts among deities. In the Enuma Elish (Babylonian creation epic), he aids in world creation and supports younger Gods.

Enki fathered several important Gods, including Marduk, who became the chief God of Babylon.
He is often depicted as a bearded figure with flowing water and fish emanating from his shoulders, symbolising his dominion over water.

He is sometimes shown with a goat and fish, representing fertility and water.

Poseidon in Greek Mythology

Poseidon, a major figure among the Twelve Olympian Gods, is best known as the God of the Sea, but he also ruled over earthquakes, storms, and horses. Depicted with his iconic trident, Poseidon was both revered and feared for his control over oceans and natural disasters.

Poseidon controlled all bodies of water. Sailors prayed to him for safe passage, while storms and shipwrecks were attributed to his anger.

Known as the *"Earth-Shaker,"* Poseidon could cause earthquakes and violent sea storms, reflecting his volatile temperament.

Poseidon was associated with horses, credited with creating the first horse and revered by horsemen and charioteers. He is often depicted riding a chariot pulled by horses across the sea.

He was one of three sons of the Titans Cronus and Rhea, alongside Zeus (king of the Gods) and Hades (God of the Underworld). After overthrowing Cronus, they divided the cosmos: Zeus took the sky, Hades the underworld, and Poseidon the seas.
However, Cronos was nothing to do with Poseidon. I have a documentary on my website that has complete evidence: www.ourtruehistory.co.uk

Poseidon married the sea nymph Amphitrite, who became his queen. They had children, including Triton, a merman who calmed or raised waves with a conch shell.

He had numerous lovers, fathering figures like Theseus (a hero), Pegasus (the winged horse), and Polyphemus (the Cyclops in The Odyssey).

Poseidon antagonises Odysseus after he blinds Polyphemus, Poseidon's son, prolonging Odysseus' journey with sea-related challenges.

Poseidon initially supported the Greeks but grew angry when they failed to honour him for building Troy's walls, reflecting his fluctuating loyalties.

Poseidon's trident, his most recognisable symbol, could create storms, cause earthquakes, or calm seas.

He is often depicted with dolphins, fish, and horses, symbolising his control over sea and land.

Poseidon is shown riding a chariot pulled by sea creatures or horses, showcasing his dominance.

Neptune in Roman Mythology

Neptune, the Roman God of the sea, closely parallels Poseidon but holds a distinct place in Roman religion and culture. He governed oceans, rivers, freshwater, and horses, and was a principal deity in the Roman pantheon.

Neptune ruled all waters, revered by sailors and fishermen for safe travels and bountiful fishing. He could calm or unleash storms and waves.
He was worshipped as the creator of horses and patron of horse racing, honoured during the Neptunalia festival with games and races.

He was the brother of Jupiter (Zeus) and Pluto (Hades). After overthrowing their father Saturn (Cronus), they divided the cosmos: Jupiter took the heavens, Neptune the seas, and Pluto the underworld.

Neptune married Salacia, a sea Goddess akin to Amphitrite, representing calm waters. They ruled the marine domain and had children like Triton, a messenger of the sea.

Celebrated on July 23 during the hottest, driest time of year, Romans prayed to Neptune for rain and water, holding outdoor feasts and games.

Neptune's trident symbolised his power over water and sea creatures.

He is depicted with sea horses, dolphins, and fish, often riding a chariot pulled by these creatures.

- **Enki:** Appears in Sumerian texts around 3500–3000 BCE.
- **Poseidon:** Emerges in Greek mythology around 1500–1200 BCE (~2000 years after Enki).
- **Neptune:** Appears in Roman mythology around 400–300 BCE (~800–900 years after Poseidon, ~2600–2700 years after Enki).

The British Museum and Encyclopaedia Britannica confirm Poseidon and Neptune are the same God across Greek and Roman cultures.

Shared Characteristics of Enki, Poseidon, and Neptune:

- **Enki** (freshwater, Abzu) and Poseidon/Neptune (sea) are central deities of water.
- **Enki** is linked to life creation, while Poseidon/Neptune are associated with fertility through water's life-giving properties.
- **Enki** influences the earth via freshwater, while Poseidon/Neptune, as *"Earth-Shakers,"* cause earthquakes.
- **Enki** brought wisdom and civilisation; Poseidon/Neptune, though primarily sea Gods, are linked to founding cities (e.g., Poseidon as patron of Corinth).
- **Enki** created various beings; Poseidon/Neptune are credited with creating horses and sea creatures.
- All three have temperamental personalities, reflecting water's unpredictability.
- **Enki** resolves disputes among Gods; Poseidon/Neptune are involved in mythological conflicts and negotiations.

The trident is a defining symbol of Poseidon and Neptune. Interestingly, tridents appear in Sumerian carvings predating Greek and Roman Gods.

Could the Greeks and Romans have seen Enki with a trident and adopted it? While this shows the Anunnaki used tridents first, it is not conclusive evidence.

Sumerian carving on an Anunnaki with a Trident!

Poseidon is credited with creating the first horse, either for Demeter or in competition with Athena for Athens' patronage. He also fathered Pegasus, the winged horse, born from Medusa's blood. Horses are sacred to Poseidon, depicted pulling his chariot.

In the Atrahasis tablet, Enki is linked to *"lahmu-creatures"* from Mars (Lahmu), which I suggested in another video could be horses.

The text states:
*"As for the bolt that bars the sea,
Ea with his lahmu-creatures shall keep it locked.
He ordered, and Anu and Adad kept the (air) above (earth) locked. And:
Ellil made his voice heard
And [spoke] to the vizier Nusku, 'Have the fifty (?) lahmu-heroes (?) ... fetched for me! ...'
The fifty (?) lahmu-heroes (?) were fetched for him."*

I propose these *"lahmu-creatures"* were horses from Mars, distinct from modern horses, with sloped backs.

The Anunnaki may have genetically modified them into the domesticated kunga, a hybrid of a female donkey and male Syrian wild ass, found only in Mesopotamia.

A Science Advances article (January 14, 2022) confirms:
"The equid bones unearthed at Umm el-Marra were hybrids, probably the mythical kungas, the earliest-known hybrids developed by humans. ... Kungas were strong, fast, and sterile hybrids of a female domestic donkey and a male Syrian wild ass."

The Standard of Ur (4600 years old) depicts kungas pulling battle chariots, and Assyrian records show their continued use. These kungas, dated to 3000–2000 BCE at Tell Umm el-Marra, align with the Anunnaki's presence in Mesopotamia.

A Washington Post article further supports this:
"Around 4,200 years ago, one particular lineage of horse quickly became dominant across Eurasia, suggesting that's when humans started to spread domesticated horses. ... It had a genetic mutation that changed the shape of its back, likely making it easier to ride."

Mainstream claims this was a natural mutation, but a single mutation would not affect all horses unless deliberately spread. The article adds:
"Humans changed the horse genome stunningly quickly, perhaps because we already had experience dealing with animals," said Laurent Frantz.

This suggests genetic manipulation, similar to how the Anunnaki created the domesticated pig (see my videos on my website). Enki, known for genetic creation, likely engineered these horses before Poseidon's myths emerged.

Poseidon fathered Polyphemus, the Cyclops in The Odyssey. Cyclops-like figures appear in Sumerian art, such as a seal from Uruk (3400–3000 BCE) depicting a one-eyed hero holding lions. While I found no direct link between Enki and a Cyclops, There are sumerian carvings of Cyclops with Anunnaki!

Nergal (Son of Enki) and a Cyclops

Cyclopia (a real condition involving a single eye) predates Greek myths and appears in Mesopotamia, where Enki was prominent.

There is a cylinder seal that also has a cyclops and is the he first-known depiction of a cyclops, and was carved into this seal from the Sumerian city of Uruk.

Poseidon is credited with creating Pegasus and other creatures like centaurs, griffins, and minotaurs.

Sumerians had all those hybrid creatures first

These creatures appear in Mesopotamian art before Greek mythology, suggesting they originated where the Anunnaki, including Enki, were active.

While not directly tied to Enki, his role in creating humans supports his capacity for such creations.

Neptune, appearing later, lacks creation myths but is associated with the same creatures as Poseidon, reinforcing the continuity between Poseidon and Neptune.

Enki and Enlil mirror Poseidon and Zeus. Enlil, the younger brother, led as Zeus did, despite Enki (like Poseidon) being older. This parallel strengthens the Enki-Poseidon connection.

In the Greek myth of Deucalion and Pyrrha, Zeus sends a flood to destroy humanity. Prometheus warns his son Deucalion to build a boat. In my Enlil chapter, I showed Enlil (Zeus) planned the flood, while Enki opposed it, as seen in the Atrahasis tablet (British Museum):
"The warrior Ellil ... 'You imposed your loads on man, ... You must ... and [create a flood]. ... Let us make far-sighted Enki swear ... an oath.'
Enki made his voice heard
And spoke to his brother Gods, 'Why should I use my power against my people?

The flood that you mention ... What is it? I don't even know! Could I give birth to a flood? That is Ellil's kind of work!'"

Enki then instructs Noah (also known as Atrahasis, Ziusudra or Zi-ud-sura and Utnapishtim), his son, to build a boat. Similarly, in the Greek myth, Prometheus (they got this mixed; he aligned with Enki not another person) warns Deucalion, his son, to build a boat.

The Roman flood story in Ovid's Metamorphoses (8 CE) mirrors this, adapting the Greek tale. Enki, like Prometheus, consistently protects humanity, opposing Enlil's attempts to destroy it.

I refer to Enki, Poseidon, and Neptune as the *"Trio"* to highlight their shared identity. Their connections, water, creation, horses, temperament, and flood stories demonstrate that Enki's attributes and actions predate and align with those of Poseidon and Neptune, supporting the argument that they are the same deity across different cultures.

Chapter 3

Enlil - Which Greek and Roman God Was He?

If you have seen my video on Cronos, you know who he was as an Anunnaki.
To provide some context, Enlil was the second son of King Anu on the planet Nibiru, with a half-brother named Enki.

Despite being younger, Enlil was in line for kingship. When he arrived on Earth, he was granted full leadership. His name, possibly originally Elil on his home planet, changed to Enlil upon taking command, meaning *"Lord of the Air"* or *"Lord of the Wind"* in Sumerian, derived from *"En"* (Lord) and *"lil"* (air or wind). Some translators suggest it could also mean *"Lord Supreme."*

Enlil was a chief deity in Sumerian, Akkadian, Assyrian, and Babylonian texts. His temple, the Ekur in Nippur, was a major religious site in ancient Mesopotamia.

Enlil wielded powerful, sometimes destructive influence, sending floods or storms to punish humanity, yet he was also a protector and source of prosperity when appeased.
To identify Enlil's Greek and Roman counterparts, I propose he was Zeus in Greek mythology and Jupiter in Roman mythology. Let us examine the evidence.

In Greek Mythology

Zeus was the king of the Gods and ruler of Mount Olympus, representing the sky, thunder, lightning, law, order, and justice.

As the most powerful Olympian, he was associated with authority and kingship. Zeus wielded thunderbolts to punish wrongdoers or assert his power and maintained cosmic order, overseeing divine and human laws. He protected oaths, hospitality (xenia is an ancient Greek concept meaning *"guest-friendship"* or *"hospitality"*), and social institutions like marriage.

The Anunnaki timeline, with Anu as the last of twelve Nibiru kings (the Titans), suggests the Greek oral tradition confused the succession. Uranus, as Anu, could not have fathered earlier kings, as he was the final ruler.

Greek mythology evolved through oral traditions, written down centuries later by poets like Homer (The Iliad and The Odyssey, 8th century BCE, ~400 years after the Trojan War), Hesiod (Theogony and Works and Days, late 8th–early 7th century BCE), and later playwrights like Aeschylus, Sophocles, and Euripides (5th century BCE, ~200–300 years after Homer).

Herodotus and Plutarch (1st–2nd century CE, ~1000 years later) further adapted these stories. These gaps, spanning hundreds or thousands of years by my dating, likely introduced errors, making the written accounts unreliable.

It is widely accepted that Enki, Enlil's half-brother, was Poseidon in Greek mythology and Neptune in Roman mythology, as the God of water. If Poseidon's father was Uranus (Anu), Zeus' father should be the same. The Greek claim that Cronus fathered both Zeus and Poseidon likely stems from a single misretelling, solidified 400 years later. Uranus, as Anu, was the true father of Zeus and Poseidon.

Further evidence lies in the scarcity of Uranus' depictions in Greek art and his absence from the twelve main Olympian Gods. As King Anu, he remained on Nibiru, rarely visiting Earth, unlike Enlil, whose actions, like attempting to destroy humanity, were widely recorded in Greek stories.

The Greeks primarily documented Anu's battle with Alula (Cronus), with little else about him, as he was not on Earth to inspire grand tales.

A key parallel is Enlil's marriage story. Enlil, enamoured with a young girl named Sud, disguised himself as a bird, seduced her, and fathered her child. Forced to marry her, Sud became Ninlil.

In Greek mythology, Zeus, infatuated with Europa, a Phoenician princess, transformed into a white bull to approach her. Enchanted, Europa climbed onto his back, and Zeus carried her to Crete, where he revealed his identity and seduced her. She bore him Minos, Rhadamanthus, and Sarpedon.

The similarities suggest these stories describe the same event.

Enlil was associated with a great flood in the Sumerian Atrahasis epic, decreeing humanity's destruction due to their noise and behaviour. Similarly, Zeus, in the Greek myth of Deucalion and Pyrrha, flooded the Earth to eliminate corrupt Bronze Age humans, with Deucalion and Pyrrha surviving to repopulate by throwing stones that became people. This flood narrative, also present in biblical accounts, ties Enlil to Zeus.

Enlil sometimes sent plagues and diseases as punishment, while Zeus punished figures like Prometheus for stealing fire or gave Pandora to Epimetheus, unleashing troubles on humanity. As a storm and agriculture deity, Enlil controlled natural elements harshly, much like Zeus, who unleashed storms, thunder, and lightning to punish or respond to human actions.

The Prometheus myth further aligns Enlil with Zeus. In Greek mythology, Prometheus (Enki) shaped humans from clay, with Athena breathing life into them. To aid weak humans, he stole fire from the Gods, defying Zeus, who punished him by binding him to a rock where an eagle ate his liver daily.

In the Sumerian Atrahasis epic, Enki, not Prometheus, proposed creating humans from clay, mixed with a slain God's flesh and blood, to relieve the Gods' labour.

In the Enki and Ninmah tablet, Enki and Ninmah shaped humans from clay, and in the Eridu Genesis, Nintur formed humans from clay to serve the Gods.

These accounts, predating Greek myths, suggest Prometheus' role aligns with Enki, not Enlil. Enlil, angered by humans' intelligence, mirrors Zeus' frustration with Prometheus. Since Poseidon (Enki) was Zeus' brother, not Prometheus, the Greek stories likely misattributed Enki's actions to Prometheus.

Greek sources, like Hesiod's Theogony and Homer's epics, consistently depict Zeus and Poseidon as brothers, sons of Cronus and Rhea, ruling the sky and sea, respectively.

However, regional variations and narrative needs introduced inconsistencies, such as differing roles in the Titanomachy. Prometheus' myths vary more, with his motivations ranging from noble to rebellious, and his role in human creation sometimes attributed to other deities. These discrepancies reflect Greek mythology's fluid, regionally diverse nature, unlike the more consistent Sumerian clay tablets.

In Sumerian mythology, the cosmos was divided among Anu, Enlil, and Enki. Anu ruled the heavens, Enlil oversaw Earth's land and people, and Enki controlled water and wisdom, based in the Abzu (Africa), later associated with Ereshkigal and Nergal's underworld, akin to Hades' realm. These divisions parallel the Greek split among Zeus (sky), Poseidon (sea), and Hades (underworld), with Nergal as Hades.

In Roman Mythology

Jupiter, the chief God, mirrors Zeus. Jupiter ruled the sky and thunder, wielding lightning bolts, and was married to Juno (Hera in Greek), overseeing justice and law.

His symbols, lightning bolt, eagle, and oak tree match Zeus', as do his roles in divine and mortal conflicts, such as the Titanomachy, and his fatherhood of Gods like Mars and heroes like Hercules. Jupiter's great flood to punish human corruption, as described in Roman mythology, aligns with Enlil's and Zeus' flood narratives.

Among other Roman Gods, such as Neptune (Poseidon), Mars (Ares), or Pluto (Hades), none match Enlil's profile as closely as Jupiter. King Anu, who rarely visited Earth, aligns with Uranus, not Jupiter, leaving Enlil as Jupiter's Sumerian counterpart.

The flood narrative, central to Enlil, Zeus, and Jupiter, is a defining link. No other Greek or Roman God fits Enlil's role as a supreme, storm-wielding, punitive yet protective deity. Thus, Enlil was Zeus in Greek mythology and Jupiter in Roman mythology, with his stories adapted across cultures over time.

Chapter 4

Inanna: The Mesopotamian Goddess and Her Legacy

Inanna, the ancient Mesopotamian Goddess of love, war, and fertility, whose legacy resonates through history, connecting to Greek and Roman mythology.

Inanna's story is one of complexity, power, and celestial significance, tied to the planet Venus and revered across cultures under various names, such as Ishtar and Astarte.

Inanna, a central figure in Sumerian mythology, was the granddaughter of Enlil, a prominent Anunnaki God. Her parents were Nanna, the moon God, and Ningal, his consort. She had a sister, Ereshkigal, ruler of the underworld, and a twin brother, Utu.

Known for her multifaceted nature, Inanna embodied love, sexuality, fertility, and war. A Goddess who was both passionate and fierce; she established a brothel, yet was known to wield power ruthlessly, even cutting off heads in her pursuit of dominance.

Her name, derived from Sumerian, is often interpreted as *"Lady of Heaven"* (Nin-anna, where Nin means *"Lady"* and Anna means *"Heaven"*). In Akkadian, she was called Ishtar, a name adopted by later Mesopotamian cultures like the Assyrians and Babylonians.
This evolution of her name reflects the fluidity of Anunnaki naming practices, where a single name encapsulated a deity's identity, much like Native American names such as Cherokee's *"Eternal Blossom"* or Hopi's *"Brown Hills."*

Over time, Inanna's identity extended to other cultures as Astarte in Canaanite and Phoenician traditions, carrying her attributes of love and fertility.

Inanna's epithets further highlight her divine roles:
- Queen of Heaven: Emphasising her celestial domain.
- Morning and Evening Star: Reflecting her association with Venus.
- Lady of Love and War: Capturing her dual nature.
- Great Lady of Heaven (Nin-ara): Used in Sumerian hymns.
- Mother of the Herds: Symbolising fertility and abundance.
- Lady of the Date Clusters: Tied to agricultural fertility.
- Shepherdess of the People: Denoting her protective role.
- Lady of the Battlefield: Highlighting her martial prowess.
- Storm Bird: Representing her fierce, unpredictable nature.
- Lioness of Heaven (Lebatu): Symbolising strength and dominance, often depicted with lions.

Her connection to Venus, the planet, is profound. Ancient texts, such as the Venus Tablet of Ammisaduqa from the mid-17th century BCE, record detailed observations of Venus, referring to it as the *"Bright Queen of the Sky"* or *"Bright Queen of Heaven"*, titles that align with Inanna's celestial identity.

Inanna's association with Venus is reinforced by her symbols, notably the eight-pointed star, a common representation of the planet in Mesopotamian art and texts.

Her epithet Lebatu connected her to lions; she had them as pets. These symbols carried across cultures, linking her to later deities and reinforcing her enduring influence.

Inanna and Lucifer

A fascinating, albeit speculative, interpretation connects Inanna to the figure of Lucifer, derived from Isaiah 14:12 in the King James Version: *"How art thou fallen from heaven, O Lucifer, son of the morning? How art thou cut down to the ground, which didst weaken the nations?"*

This passage, often associated with the fall of Satan in Christian tradition, may have deeper roots in Mesopotamian mythology.

The Hebrew word helel ben shahar translates to *"shining one, son of the dawn"* or *"morning star,"* a clear reference to Venus.

Given Inanna's exclusive association with Venus as the morning and evening star. I have a video on my website showing who Lucifer was!
I am the only person to have worked it out, as with many other things that are not in these books. You can see the videos on my website: www.ourtruehistory.co.uk

Inanna's Legacy in Greek and Roman Mythology

Inanna's attributes and celestial connections find clear parallels in the Roman Goddess Venus and the Greek Goddess Aphrodite, with a less likely connection to Athena. Let us explore these relationships.

Venus: The Roman Counterpart

Venus, the Roman Goddess of love, beauty, and fertility, shares striking similarities with Inanna:

- Domain: Both govern love, sexuality, and fertility, embodying desire and passion.
- Planetary Association: Both are directly tied to the planet Venus, symbolising the morning and evening star.
- Symbols: Inanna's eight-pointed star and Venus's radiance reflect their shared celestial identity.
- Dual Nature: While Venus is primarily known for love, her role as Venus Victrix (Venus the Victorious) connects her to military success, mirroring Inanna's warlike aspect. Venus's affair with Mars, the God of war, parallels Inanna's dual role in love and conflict.

Aphrodite: The Greek Equivalent

Aphrodite, the Greek Goddess of love, beauty, fertility, and desire, is an even closer match to Inanna:
- Shared Domains: Both Goddesses are central to love, beauty, and fertility. Inanna's sacred marriage rituals, which celebrated abundance, mirror Aphrodite's dominion over romantic and sexual love.
- Venus Connection: Both are associated with the planet Venus, reinforcing their symbolic link as the morning and evening star.
- Passionate Nature: Aphrodite's role in the Trojan War, sparking conflict through her beauty, parallels Inanna's capacity for destruction driven by emotion. Both are portrayed as bold, passionate, and occasionally vengeful.
- Cultural Influence: Inanna's worship influenced later cultures, such as the Canaanites (via Astarte) and Phoenicians, which in turn shaped Greek religion. Aphrodite likely inherited traits from these earlier Mesopotamian Goddesses.

Aphrodite's associations with doves, roses, and the myrtle tree, as well as her relationships with figures like Adonis and Ares (the Greek equivalent of Mars), further align her with Inanna's themes of love and conflict.

Athena: An Unlikely Match

While Athena, the Greek Goddess of wisdom, strategy, and warfare, shares Inanna's martial aspect, she is an unlikely counterpart:
- Warfare Style: Athena represents strategic, defensive warfare, emphasising intellect and order. Inanna, by contrast, embodies chaotic, passionate warfare driven by ambition and emotion.
- Wisdom vs. Cunning: Athena's wisdom is rational, while Inanna's intelligence is cunning and power-driven.
- Virginity vs. Sexuality: Athena is a virgin Goddess, detached from love and fertility, whereas Inanna is deeply tied to eroticism and passion. Depictions of Inanna, Ishtar, Venus, and Aphrodite often emphasise their sensuality, unlike Athena's modest portrayal.

While Athena may resemble Inanna in her warlike nature, her lack of connection to love and fertility makes her an incomplete match. The Statue of Liberty, often linked to Athena due to its symbolism of wisdom and freedom, further underscores this distinction.

It seems to me Inanna was also Venus and Aphrodite.

Chapter 5

Dragons

Welcome to an exploration of dragons. You might be thinking, why dragons in this book about Almighty God?

Well, dragons were mentioned in the Bible... and guess who first mentioned dragons!

These iconic figures are woven into the mythologies of cultures worldwide. From the legend of St. George and the Dragon to the Chinese Dragon Kings, these creatures captivate our imagination with their fiery breath, immense size, and otherworldly presence. But what lies at the heart of these stories?

This chapter delves into the origins of dragon myths, tracing them back to ancient Sumerian texts and proposing that dragons were not winged reptiles but celestial phenomena, comets, interpreted as living entities by ancient civilisations like the Anunnaki.

In Christian mythology, the tale of St. George slaying a dragon in the 3rd or 4th century symbolises triumph over evil. The Germanic epic Nibelungenlied (13th century) features Fafnir, a dragon embodying greed in Norse mythology's Poetic Edda.

Slavic folklore tells of Dobrynya Nikitich battling a dragon, while Chinese mythology reveres Dragon Kings as celestial beings controlling weather. These tales, among countless others, raise the question: why are dragons so universal?

To uncover the origins of dragons, we must turn to the oldest texts, those from Sumeria, home of the Anunnaki Gods. The Anunnaki viewed celestial bodies, planets, comets, and asteroids as living entities with personalities and emotions.

In their cosmology, *"heaven"* referred to space, not a divine realm. Thus, a dragon in heaven was a cosmic phenomenon, not a winged creature soaring through the heavens.

Sumerian texts describe dragons as long fire-emitting beings associated with celestial Gods like Enki and Ninurta, who governed cosmic and natural order.
For example, in **Enki and the World Order** (c. 1113),

Enki is called the *"Great Dragon who stands in Eridug, whose shadow covers Heaven and Earth."* Eridug situates this dragon as a cosmic entity. The dragon's *"shadow"* over heaven and earth suggests a celestial body casting a visible effect, like a comet's glowing tail.

Comets, with their brilliant glow and dust streams, align closely with descriptions of dragons emitting light or fire when entering the atmosphere of Earth. Their association with catastrophic events, such as meteor impacts, explains the dragon's link to chaos and devastation.

In The Song of the Hoe (c. 55.4), Ninurta (son of Enlil), armed by Enlil with weapons like a mace and arrows, battles a dragon called Ushumgal, which *"roars like a storm"* and *"strikes"* toward Earth.

This imagery evokes a comet or asteroid entering the atmosphere and a spaceship with weapons firing at it.

The Enuma Elish, a Babylonian creation epic, describes Tiamat as a planet, with smaller rocks beside it.

Here from the Enuma Elish :

"Ummu-Hubur [Tiamat] who formed all things, made in addition weapons invincible; she spawned monster-serpents, sharp of tooth, and merciless of fang; with poison, instead of blood, she filled their bodies. Fierce monster-vipers she clothed with terror."

Yes, the Anunnaki used the word serpent for something or someone they did not like; it is like us calling someone a bad name or swear word. Yes, the serpent that told Adam and Eve was an Anunnaki, he wanted Adam and Eve dead because Enki had bred with humans and that changed the bloodline of the Dingir - Gods. Please watch my video on Adam and Eve on my website.

In the ancient texts, one text noting a dragon 50 beru (approximately 300–350 miles) long, its head rising six to seven miles.
Such scale suggests a cosmic entity, not a biological creature. The dragon's *"blood"* flowing for three years after being slain aligns with a comet's tail or debris dispersing over time. Tiamat's creations, including scorpion men and hurricanes, reinforce the idea of dragons as cosmic forces, not earthly reptiles.

Dragons and Catastrophic Events

Dragon myths often tie to destruction, a theme echoed in their celestial origins.

The Chaldean Account of Genesis (1876) describes a seven-headed serpent stirring the sea into waves, identified as *"the chaos of the deep"* or *"the serpent of night."* The *"deep"* here refers to space, where water exists in cometary ice and vapour.

This serpent's actions may symbolise cosmic events like meteor showers or impacts, which ancient cultures interpreted as battles between Gods and monsters. For instance, the story of seven *"wicked spirits"* attacking the moon likely reflects attempts to explain lunar eclipses, similar to Chinese beliefs that a dragon devours the moon during an eclipse.

In Ninurta's Return to Nibru (c. 1.61), Ninurta brings forth a *"warrior dragon"* from the mountains and other creatures from cosmic realms, suggesting a celestial object that crashed to Earth; its remains prized as a relic and possibly now part of it is the *"Mecca stone"*, which refers to the Black Stone (al-Ḥajar al-Aswad), an important Islamic relic set in the eastern corner of the Kaaba in Mecca, Saudi Arabia.

The text Letter from Amar-Sin to Shulgi (c. 3.21) describes dragons killing and leaving devastation, with fire consuming reed beds despite waterways, evoking the fiery impact of a meteor igniting the landscape.

These accounts suggest that catastrophic celestial events, comets or asteroids striking Earth, their fire and destruction immortalised as *"fire-breathing"* beasts.

Evolution of Dragon Imagery

While early dragon myths focused on celestial phenomena, their depictions evolved.

In Mesopotamian and Greek mythologies, dragons like parts of Tiamat or the Hydra were serpentine, wingless creatures.

The Mushussu from Mesopotamian lore, a dragon-like creature, lacked wings but shared traits with comets, such as a long body and fearsome appearance.

No Anunnaki called the Mushussu a dragon, because it was an animal that Marduk had as a pet, but in modern times we call that pet a dragon, because we are thick!

The iconic winged, fire-breathing dragon emerged later, notably in the Old English epic Beowulf (8th–11th centuries), where a dragon guards treasure and battles the hero to their mutual demise. This portrayal shaped Western dragon lore, establishing the archetype of a winged, fiery beast.

Why did wings become a feature? For thousands of years, dragons were depicted without them, resembling comets with long, fiery tails. The addition of wings, prominent in medieval European mythology, may have drawn from the fact that comets when entering Earth's atmosphere fly across the sky with a fire tail.

The Roman Draco Standard (2nd century CE), a dragon-shaped military emblem sometimes depicted with wings, and the Lindworm of later European folklore, a two-legged winged dragon, reflect this shift. These creative choices transformed dragons into hybrid creatures, blending celestial origins with earthly fears.

Let us look at any other ways a dragon could have been real or at least described as we know today.

Could dragons have biological roots? While no creature matches the mythical dragon's six appendages (four legs, two wings), and no skeletons have even been found, certain animals may have inspired their traits:

- **Bombardier Beetle:** Ejects a boiling chemical spray, resembling fire-spitting.
- **Electric Eel:** Generates electricity, akin to emitting a harmful force.
- **Spitting Cobra:** Sprays venom with accuracy, evoking dragon-like attacks.
- **Bioluminescent Sea Creatures:** Emit glowing light, likened to fire in dark settings.

These traits, observed by ancient peoples, could have fuelled dragon legends, though no known animal fits the full mythical description, as six appendages defy tetrapod evolution.

Fossils likely played a role. Discoveries of dinosaur or pterosaur remains, mistaken for dragon bones, may have inspired myths. For example:
- **Pterosaurs:** Flying reptiles like Quetzalcoatlus (with a 40-foot wingspan) or Rhamphorhynchus (with a long tail and sharp teeth) resemble dragons in form.
- **Spinosaurus:** A semi-aquatic dinosaur with a crocodile-like snout and sail-like back, evoking sea or swamp dragons.
- **Dracorex hogwartsia:** A small dinosaur with a spiky, dragon-like skull, its name meaning *"Dragon King of Hogwarts."*
- **Early Fossil Finds:** Large, unusual bones could have been interpreted as dragon remains, fuelling speculation.

While these creatures share dragon-like traits, none breathed fire.

Dragon imagery varies by culture, reflecting local interpretations of celestial and natural phenomena.

The Chinese knew exactly what a dragon was; it was a comet, just like the Anunnaki spoke about as a dragon.

In Chinese tradition, the dragon is not merely a creature of legend but a celestial presence, a bridge between heaven and earth. Unlike the fearsome, treasure-hoarding dragons of the West, the Chinese dragon embodies the forces of nature and the rhythms of the cosmos.

Dragons were believed to inhabit the skies, riding the currents of air and water, and their forms were often tied to specific celestial phenomena, such as the Azure Dragon of the East, one of the Four Symbols that govern the cardinal directions and the seasons. In this way, the dragon becomes a cosmic guardian, a living embodiment of heaven's authority on earth, capable of guiding rulers, protecting the land, and maintaining the delicate harmony of nature itself.

Over time, the term *"dragon"* became a catch-all for various phenomena, much like *"demon"* denotes evil.

The first people to even use the word were the Anunnaki and they were talking about comets.

Sumerian texts portray dragons as radiant, destructive forces in the heavens, their immense size and fiery trails evoking comets or meteors.

Catastrophic events, like impacts or eclipses, fuelled myths of Gods battling dragons, while fossils and natural phenomena, such as volcanic eruptions or bioluminescent creatures, added layers to their imagery.

Over centuries, dragons evolved from wingless, cosmic serpents to the winged, fire-breathing beasts of medieval lore, shaped by cultural creativity and the human need to explain the unexplainable.

Here is just some of the ancient texts translated that have the word dragon. If you want to look them up, here are the titles; I am sure you will agree it was a comet.

- The Epic of Creation (Enuma Elish)
- The Epic of Gilgamesh
- The Book of Isaiah
- The Book of Jeremiah
- The Book of Ezekiel
- The Book of Psalms
- The Book of Nehemiah
- The Baal Cycle
- The Avesta
- The Shahnameh (Book of Kings)
- The Myth of Illuyanka
- The Myth of Anzu
- Bel and the Dragon

Chapter 6

Anunnaki Created Us Twice

We need to first look at when they first created us, and then see what they said and why. Forgive me if you already know the story, but I have to go through this carefully, because if I am right, then it changes everything we know about humans.

The Sumerian text Enki and Ninmah is preserved on several clay tablets housed in various museum collections.

- Penn Museum, Philadelphia, tablet **CBS 2168**. This Old Babylonian period tablet excavated from Nippur contains a fragment of the Enki and Ninmah.
- Penn Museum tablet **CBS 4561**. Also from Nippur, this tablet features the myth of Enki and Ninhursag, which shares thematic elements with Enki and Ninmah.
- Louvre Museum, Paris, tablet **AO 7036**. This tablet includes the Enki and Ninmah story.

These tablets, inscribed with cuneiform script, date back to the Old Babylonian period, circa 1900 to 1600 BCE, and were primarily discovered in the ancient city of Nippur, a significant religious centre in Mesopotamia.

Here is the translation in full from the Enki and Ninmah tablets:

"In those days, in the days when heaven and earth were created, in those nights, in the nights when heaven and earth were created, in those years, in the years when the fates were determined, when the Anuna Gods were born, when the Goddesses were taken in marriage, when the Goddesses were distributed in heaven and earth, when the Goddesses became pregnant and gave birth, when the Gods were obliged their food for their meals. The senior Gods oversaw the work, while the minor Gods were bearing the toil. The Gods were digging the canals and piling up the silt in Harali. The Gods, dredging the clay, began complaining about this life.

At that time, the one of great wisdom, the creator of all the senior Gods, Enki, lay on his bed, not waking up from his sleep, in the deep anger, in the flowing water, the place the inside of which no other God knows. The Gods said, weeping, 'He is the cause of the lamenting.' Namma, the primeval mother who gave birth to the senior Gods, took the tears of the Gods to the one who lay sleeping, to the one who did not wake up from his bed, to her son. 'Are you really lying there asleep and not awake? The Gods, your creatures, are smashing there. My son, wake up from your bed. Please apply the skill deriving from your wisdom and create a substitute, for the Gods so that they can be freed from their toil.'

"At the word of his mother Namma, Enki rose up from his bed. In Halankug, his room for pondering, he slapped his thigh in annoyance.

The wise and intelligent one, the prudent, of skills, the fashioner of the design of everything brought to life birth Goddesses.

Enki reached out his arm over them and turned his attention to them.

And after Enki, the fashioner of designs by himself had pondered the matter, he said to his mother, Namma, 'My mother, the creature you planned will really come into existence.

Impose on him the work of carrying baskets, you should need clay from the top of the Abzu. The birth Goddesses will nip off the clay and you shall bring the form into existence. Let Ninmah act as your assistant and let Ninmah, Kuziana, Ninmada, Ninbarag, Ninmug, and Ninguna stand by as you give birth. My mother, after you have decreed his fate, let Ninmah impose on him the work of carrying baskets.'

Six lines fragmentary Enki brought joy to their heart. He set a feast for his mother, Namma, and for Ninmah. All the princely birth Goddesses, eight delicate reed and bread, and Enlil and the Lord Nudimmud roasted holy kids. All the senior Gods praised him. 'Oh Lord of wide understanding, who is as wise as you?

Enki, the great Lord, who can equal your actions. Like a corporeal father, you are the one who has the me of deciding destinies. In fact, you are the me.'

Enki and Ninmah drank beer. Their hearts became elated. And then Ninmah said to Enki, 'Man's body can be either good or bad. And whether I make a fate good or bad depends on my will.' Enki answered Ninmah, 'I will counterbalance whatever fate, good or bad, you happen to decide.

' Ninmah took clay from the top of the Abzu in her hand, and she fashioned from it first a man who could not bend his outstretched weak hands.

Enki looked at the man who could not bend his outstretched weak hands and decreed his fate. He appointed him as a servant of the king.

Second, she fashioned one who turned back, the light, a man with constantly opened eyes. Enki looked at the one who turned back, the light, the man with constantly opened eyes, and decreed his fate allotting to it the musical arts, making him as the chief in the king's presence.

Third, she fashioned one with both feet broken, one with paralyzed feet. Enki looked at the one with both feet broken, the one with paralyzed feet and him for the work of, and the silversmith and worse, Mrs. Has instead. She fashioned one, a third one born as an idiot. Enki looked at this one, the one born as an idiot and decreed his fate. He appointed him as a servant of the king.

Fourth, she fashioned one who could not hold back his urine. Enki looked at the one who could not hold back his urine and bathed him in enchanted water and drove out the Namtar demon from his body.

Fifth, she fashioned a woman who could not give birth. Enki looked at the woman who could not give birth and decreed her fate. He made her belong to the queen's household. As a weaver, fashioned her to belong to the queen's household.

She fashioned one with neither penis nor vagina on its body. Enki looked at the one with neither penis nor vagina on its body and gave it the name, Nibru, eunuch, and decreed as its fate to stand before the king.

Ninmah threw the pinched off clay from her hand on the ground and a great silence fell.

The great Lord Enki said to Ninmah, 'I have decreed the fates of your creatures and given them their daily bread. Come. Now I will fashion somebody for you and you must decree the fate of the newborn one.

Enki devised a shape with head and mouth in its middle and said to Ninmah, 'Pour ejaculated semen into a woman's womb and the woman will give birth to the semen of her womb.' Ninmah stood by for the newborn and the woman brought forth in the midst. In return, this was Umal. Its head was afflicted, its place of, was afflicted.

Its eyes were afflicted, its neck was afflicted. It could hardly breathe, its ribs were shaky, its lungs were afflicted, its heart was afflicted, its bowels were afflicted. With its hand and its lolling head, it could not put bread into its mouth.
Its spine and head were dislocated. The weak hips and the shaky feet could not carry it on the field. Enki fashioned it in this way.
Enki said to Ninmah, 'For your creatures I have decreed a fate, I have given them their daily bread. Now you should decree a fate for my creature, give him his daily bread too.' Ninmah looked at Umal and turned to him.

She went nearer to Umal, asked him questions, but he could not speak. She offered him bread to eat, but he could not reach out for it. He could not lie on, he could not.

Standing up, he could not sit down, could not lie down, he could not. A house, he could not eat bread.
Ninmah answered Enki, 'The man you have fashioned is neither alive nor dead.

He cannot support himself.' Enki answered Ninmah, 'I decreed a fate for the first man with the weak hands, I gave him bread.
I decreed a fate for the man who turned back, the light, I gave him bread. I decreed a fate for the man with broken paralyzed feet, I gave him bread. I decreed a fate for the man who could not hold back his urine, I gave him bread.

I decreed a fate for the woman who could not give birth, I gave her bread. I decreed the fate for the one with neither penis nor vagina on its body, I gave it bread. My sister.'
Two lines fragmentary Ninmah answered Enki, nine lines fragmentary.

Ninmah's answer continues, 'You entered. Look, you do not dwell in heaven, you do not dwell on earth, you do not come out to look at the land. Where you do not dwell but where my house is built your words cannot be heard. Where you do not live but where my city is built, I myself am silenced.

My city is ruined, my house is destroyed, my child has been taken captive. I am a fugitive who has had to leave the ecore, even I myself could not escape from your hand.'

Enki replied to Ninmah, 'Who could change the words that left your mouth? Remove Umal from your lap. Ninmah, may your work be you? For me, what is imperfect?

Who can oppose this, the man whom I shaped after you? Let him pray. Today let my penis be praised, may your wisdom be confirmed. May the Enkam and Ninkam proclaim your glory. My sister, the heroic strength, the song, the writing, the Gods who heard, let Umal build my house. Ninmah could not rival the great Lord Enki. Father Enki, your praise is sweet.'"

When did this happen? My research based on the time frame the Anunnaki Gods used would have been about 300,000 years ago, but if you look at the dates mainstream have they are all over the place:
"For me, Homo sapiens evolved between 1 million and 700,000 years ago in Africa," John Hawks, a paleoanthropologist at the University of Wisconsin–Madison, told Live Science in an email.

Or

Discovery magazine, by Nathaniel Scharping:
"DNA evidence drawn from comparisons of different human genomes, as well as those of close cousins like Neanderthals and Denisovans, put the split between the three groups at at least 400,000 years ago. So it's possible that H. sapiens is over half a million years old."

However,
In the last two days there has been a series on the BBC, paleoanthropologist Ella Al-Shamahi reveals *"The oldest fossils that are recognisably our species, Homo sapiens, come from Jebel Irhoud in Morocco, North Africa and date back to around 300,000 years ago."*

Let us look at these other tablets Atra-hasis, the translations of the lead up to the same event:

"Ea made his voice heard and spoke to the Gods, his brothers, 'Why are we blaming them?

Their work was too hard, their trouble was too much. Every day the earth resounded.

The warning signal was loud enough, we kept hearing the noise. There is ba, belet ili the womb, Goddess is present. Let her create primeval man so that he may bear the yoke. So that he may bear the yoke, the work of Enlil. Let man bear the load of the Gods, gap, obv.'

Belet ili, the womb Goddess is present. Let the womb Goddess create offspring, Atrahasis wam, and let man bear the load of the Gods.

They called up the Goddess, asked the midwife of the Gods, 'Wise, mummy, you are the womb Goddess to be the creator of mankind. Create primeval man, that he may bear the yoke. Let him bear the yoke, the work of Enlil. Let man bear the load of the Gods.'

Nintu made her voice heard and spoke to the great Gods. 'It is not proper for me to make him. The work is Enki's. He makes everything pure. If he gives me clay, then I will do it.' Enki made his voice heard and spoke to the great Gods. 'On the first, seventh and fifteenth of the month, I shall make a purification by washing. T

hen one God should be slaughtered, and the Gods can be purified by immersion. Nintu shall mix clay with his flesh and his blood. Then a God and a man will be mixed together in clay.'"

Here in the Atra-Hasis, we find out that the young sons of the Gods, the Igigi, were tired of doing the work for the older Gods and waged a war against the great Gods. They were counting the years of loads. For 300 years, they bore the excess, hard work, night and day. (Remember their life span is way longer than ours, 300 years would have been 1 month for them).

They groaned and blamed each other, grumbled over the masses of excavated soil. *"Six, let us confront our the chamberlain and get him to relieve us of our hard work. Come, let us carry the Lord, the counselor of Gods, the warrior from his dwelling."*

That came before the text about creating a new creature. The idea came from the fact the Igigi refused to work, so the Gods needed a worker to help the Igigi.

And so the first Homo sapiens were created. What did the first Homo sapiens look like?

They were put to work in Africa, the Anunnaki called it Abzu, that is why the first Homo sapiens skeleton was found there. We know people that live there are dark, their kids were probably the colour of the African people we have now, more brown.

We know the first Homo sapiens were in Africa and the Anunnaki tell us they put the first *"men"* to work in the Abzu, Africa. We can work out from the colour of the people there, the first ones were probably dark-skinned.

We can see from people living today there seems to be a skin colour that is better suited to hotter places.

People living near the equator develop darker skin to protect against UV damage, while those living further north or south have lighter skin to allow for better absorption of UV rays, which is necessary for vitamin D production.

The Gods' home planet is not near the sun; what colour would they be? On a distant planet out near Pluto, however, conditions would be drastically different. Sunlight would be extremely weak because Pluto is 39.5 times farther from the sun than Earth. This means UV radiation exposure would be minimal.

If their planet had an atmosphere, it might block even more of the already scarce sunlight, further reducing any exposure to UV rays. If the planet had internal energy sources, like geothermal heat, instead of relying on sunlight, the surface might be dimly lit.
Combined with the possibility of a strong magnetic field, which would shield them from cosmic radiation, there would be little reason for the evolution of dark skin.

Given these conditions, the most logical conclusion is that the Anunnaki would have pale, white, or even grayish-blue skin.
Just as humans in northern regions evolved lighter skin to absorb as much available UV as possible, beings from a distant, low-light world would likely develop pale or reflective skin. This might also explain descriptions of shining or radiant Gods in ancient texts.

As reflective or light-coloured skin can give off a glowing appearance in the right lighting conditions, it is possible that their skin could even have a metallic or silvery quality, similar to certain deep-sea creatures on Earth that exhibit reflective, shiny surfaces due to their low-light habitat.
Another possibility is that their skin might be gray or bluish, similar to how certain deep-sea creatures look in the absence of sunlight.

Creatures that live in the ocean depths have evolved gray, blue, or silver-tone skin, which could be another logical adaptation for beings from a dark, distant planet.
This might also link to modern depictions of gray aliens, as these beings are often associated with extraterrestrial life. Some might wonder if the Anunnaki could have had dark or black skin.

While it is a possibility, it is unlikely based on known biological principles. On Earth, dark skin serves to protect against the sun's UV rays, but on a distant planet with minimal exposure to UV light, there would be no evolutionary advantage to developing dark skin.

For skin to become darker, there must be an environmental trigger, typically high-intensity solar radiation. Since that would not exist near Pluto, this outcome is unlikely unless the planet had some other unique form of surface radiation that dark skin would protect against.

I have gone through every mention of skin colour for any ancient God, from Norse to Bible, and the only mentions of God being dark is when they refer to them as burnt by the sun, that would make sense if they were on Earth for hundreds of thousands of years they would get sunburnt, but the female Gods, such as in Egypt were pale, sometimes painted yellow, the females did not work out in the sun.

Historical descriptions of the Anunnaki offer some clues and might help us work out what the first and 2nd generations of genetically modified humans look like.

In ancient Sumerian texts, the Anunnaki are depicted as larger-than-life, human-like figures with flowing beards and robes. While Sumerian stone reliefs do not depict colour, the descriptions of these beings as shining or radiant may hint at light, glowing, or luminous skin.

This glowing appearance is often interpreted symbolically as divine radiance, but it could also be literal if their skin had reflective or luminous properties. Some scholars also link these descriptions to other divine beings in ancient cultures, such as the blue-skinned Hindu deities Krishna and Vishnu, suggesting that the divine glow might correspond to an otherworldly skin tone or just showing blue to represent the sky, as in sky Gods.

If we consider the biological and environmental influences, as well as the symbolic and visual depictions in ancient texts, the most logical conclusion is that the Anunnaki would have pale, white, gray, or bluish skin.

Descriptions of *"shining"* or *"radiant Gods"* in texts like the Sumerian King
List or certain Akkadian myths support the idea of luminous or reflective skin.
If we imagine them stepping onto Earth from a spacecraft, the brightness of our sun might make their skin seem to glow, adding to the *"shining ones"* narrative. This *"shining"* could have been interpreted by early humans as a divine glow or spiritual radiance.

If you watch my flood video, I show that Enki was the father to Noah. Noah is mentioned in the Book of Enoch.

Noah's mother was called Betenos or Batanash if you go by the Moorehen translations. Betenos' husband was called Lamech. Noah's father was not Lamech as shown in the Book of Enoch, where Lamech gets worried that the baby Noah did not look like him at all.

From the Book of Enoch:

"And after some days, my son Methuselah took a wife for his son Lamech, and she became pregnant by him and bore a son. And his body was white as snow and red as the blooming of a rose, and the hair of his head and his long locks were white as wool, and his eyes beautiful.

And when he opened his eyes, he lighted up the whole house like the sun, and the whole house was very bright. And thereupon he arose in the hands of the midwife, opened his mouth, and conversed with the Lord of righteousness. And his father Lamech was afraid of him and fled, and came to his father Methuselah.

And he said unto him, I have begotten a strange son, diverse from and unlike man, and resembling the sons of the God of heaven, and his nature is different, and he is not like us, and his eyes are as the rays of the sun, and his countenance is glorious.

And it seems to me that he is not sprung from me, but from the angels, and I fear that in his days a wonder may be wrought on the earth.
And now my father, I am here to petition thee and implore thee that thou mayest go to Enoch, our father, and learn from him the truth, for his dwelling place is amongst the angels.

*And when Methuselah heard the words of his son, he came to me to the ends of the earth, for he had heard that I was there, and he cried aloud, and I heard his voice, and I came to him. And I said unto him, behold, here am I my son, wherefore hast thou come to me?
And he answered and said, because of a great cause of anxiety have I come to thee, and because of a disturbing vision have I approached.*

And now my father, hear me, unto Lamech my son there hath been born a son, the like of whom there is none, and his nature is not like man's nature, and the color of his body is whiter than snow, and redder than the bloom of a rose, and the hair of his head is whiter than white wool, and his eyes are like the rays of the sun, and he opened his eyes and thereupon lighted up the whole house. And he arose in the hands of the midwife, and opened his mouth and blessed the Lord of heaven.

And his father Lamech became afraid and fled to me, and did not believe that he was sprung from him, but that he was in the likeness of the angels of heaven. And behold, I have come to thee, that thou mayest make known to me the truth."

This tells us that Lamech's skin colour, and probably that of people back then was darker skin. Remember this is before the flood, because Noah was just a baby.

Lamech was able to speak. This is because he was a descendant from Adam and Eve. They were the first children from Anunnaki and Homo sapiens and were smarter than the first homo sapiens. Lemech would have been a homo sapien-sapien.

This made Adam and Eve demigods, direct offspring from Anunnaki and Homo sapiens resulting in modern man, Homo sapiens sapiens. But their children, such as Cain, bred with Homo sapiens as there was no other Homo sapiens sapiens.

This means if Adam and Eve were pale like the Anunnaki, their lineage would end up not being pale unless they only bred with other demigods, meaning Lamech and his wife would have been dark or dark olive-skinned because of the breeding with Homo sapiens.

Let us look at what we have now:
- Anunnaki: pale skin.
- First Homo sapiens : would have been dark skin, probably black curly hair.
- Demigods, the offspring of Homo sapiens and Anunnaki: would have been pale skin, probably straight white hair.
- Demigods breeding back with Homo sapiens : would have been dark skin and black curly hair.

But there is another! The black-headed people that the Anunnaki Gods mention.
So where would the black-headed people come from that they created? They would have already seen the colour black, in the dark humans from Africa, but yet only called some humans black-headed.
Can we work out who they are from the location where they were? The term black-headed people refers to the Sumerians. The ancient inhabitants of southern Mesopotamia in what is now modern-day Iraq.

They referred to themselves as sag-giga in Sumerian, which translates to black-headed ones.

The Anunnaki then bred with the Homo sapiens 200,000 years later (100,000 years ago) according to my dates and for once mainstream seem to agree; this created the modern human, Homo sapiens sapiens.

Credo Reference
https://search.credoreference.com › articles
2 days ago — Modern humans, Homo sapiens sapiens, first appeared c.100,000 years ago.

But why could not they have been here before? What makes me think there is a new race created after the flood?
The black-headed people fashioned by the Anunnaki were the Sumerians themselves, residing in the region of Sumer in southern Mesopotamia. This area is often referred to as the land of the civilised lords, or Ki-en-gir in Sumerian. They would have been olive-skinned with straight hair.

To me, the logic would be not to create a race as smart as their demigods, see *Tale of Adapa* translations online, but for them to create the black-headed people more as underlings for their demigod children, thus putting their demigod children in power positions, such as kings and priests, while the black-headed people were just simply workers for the elites.

We can see this in the story where Inanna was granted her own land, the Indus Valley in India. She took black-headed people with her.

A Sheer Namassaga to Ninsiana for Idindagan, Idindagan

"The great Anuna Gods having bowed before them stand there with prayers and supplications and utter prayers on behalf of all the lands. My lady decrees judgements in due order for the land. Two manuscripts add the line. Inanna decides verdicts for "the land" together with Enlil, her black-headed people parade before her. "

My thoughts are they took these black-headed workers around the world, dropping them off and thus some of them bred with the local hominins in those areas. I have done a video called Anunnaki and the Amercias which backs this up.

This has also been proven by mainstream. Hominins that bred with Homo sapiens, Neanderthals, Denisovans, Homo julensis, Homo erectus, hominins that bred with hominins, Neanderthals and Denisovans, Neanderthals and unknown archaic hominins, Denisovans and unknown archaic hominins. I know that's a lot to take in, basically everyone bred with everyone.

This would explain why we have Native Americans that have the same skin colour as people in the Middle East.
The people we know today would be the Indians that were the black-headed people, dark skin but straight black hair.

It makes sense but can I show texts where the Anunnaki talk about creating them?

Here in the Atra-hassis, This is talking about the time just after the great flood happened and Enlil found out that Noah was alive and in a huge boat, I'll rewrite it again explaining what happened:

"The warrior Ellil spotted the boat And was furious with the Igigi. 'We, the great Anunna, all of us, Agreed together on an oath! No form of life should have escaped! How did any man survive the catastrophe?' Anu made his voice heard And spoke to the warrior Ellil, 'Who but Enki would do this? He made sure that the [reed hut] disclosed the order.'

Enki made his voice heard And spoke to the great gods, 'I did it, in defiance of you! I made sure life was preserved [(5 lines missing) Exact your punishment from the sinner. And whoever contradicts your order (12 lines missing) I have given vent to my feelings!' Ellil made his voice heard And spoke to far-sighted Enki, 'Come, summon Nintu the womb-goddess! Confer with each other in the assembly.

' Enki made his voice heard And spoke to the womb-goddess Nintu, 'You are the womb-goddess who decrees destinies. [ ] to the people. [Let one-third of them be] l l [Let another third of them be] In addition let there be one-third of the people, Among the people the woman who gives birth yet does Not give birth (successfully); Let there be the pasittu-demon among the people, To snatch the baby from its mother's lap. Establish ugbabtu, entu, egi~ltu-women :45 They shall be taboo, and thus control childbirth.'

What this says is:
Enlil spotted Noahs boat and was furious with the Igigi. Enlil thought the Igigi helped a human survive.

'Enlil addresses the Anunnaki, We, the great Anunna, all of us, Agreed together on an oath! No form of life should have escaped! How did any man survive the catastrophe?'

King Anu made his voice heard through a radio, he was on Nibiru and spoke to the warrior Enlil, 'Who but Enki would do this? He made sure that the [reed hut] disclosed the order.'

Enki made his voice heard and spoke to the great gods, 'I did it, in defiance of you! I made sure life was preserved [(5 lines missing) Exact your punishment from the sinner. And whoever contradicts your order (12 lines missing) I have given vent to my feelings!'

Now Enlil replies to far-sighted Enki, They have chatted about the benefits of humans and Enlil starts to think maybe they need them, but they were mostly gone because of the flood. Enlil says 'Come, summon Nintu the womb-goddess! Confer with each other in the assembly. '
Enlil is thinking about creating more, Nintu was the half sister that gave birth to the very first homo sapien. She was the chief medical officer. You might know her as Ninmah or Ninhursag or Belet-ili.

 Enki made his voice heard And spoke to the womb-goddess Nintu, 'You are the womb-goddess who decrees destinies. [ ] to the people.

[Let one-third of them be] Now sadly we don't have the missing text here, that's so important, was one third part Anunnaki? Or Part Homo sapien? or part Homo sapien-sapien?

l l [Let another third of them be] Clearly they are selecting what DNA we should have.

In addition let there be one-third of the people, Among the people the woman who gives birth yet does Not give birth (successfully); Let there be the pasittu-demon among the people, To snatch the baby from its mother's lap.
What they are talking about is RH negative blood, they would give some of the women they create the virus blood to humans, which would kill the baby in the whomb if the babies father had a different blood type, the clever part of this is that it RH negative blood skips generations.
The pasittu-demon is the virus, Demon means evil or bad. They added RH to limit our population.

Establish ugbabtu, entu, egi~ltu-women : They shall be taboo, and thus control childbirth.'
They also limited our life to 120 years, this suggests that we lived longer before the flood!

Chapter 7

The Mark of the Beast

I will be starting from the point of view that the Anunnaki were the Gods in the Bible.

First, let us see what most of the world believes the mark of the beast means.

The mark of the beast mentioned in the Bible, specifically in the Book of Revelation, is a topic that has sparked various interpretations and speculations over the centuries. Most people, particularly within Christian communities, tend to view the mark of the beast as a symbol of allegiance to a figure associated with evil, or as a sign of participation in a system opposed to God.

An interpretation is that the mark of the beast represents a mechanism for economic or social exclusion where those who refuse to receive the mark are marginalised or persecuted, unable to participate in society or commerce.

Many see the mention of the mark of the beast in the Book of Revelation as part of End Times prophecy, signalling the culmination of human history and the onset of final judgment and divine intervention.

There is ongoing debate among scholars and believers regarding whether the mark of the beast should be interpreted literally as a physical mark or identifier or symbolically, representing broader spiritual or ideological concepts.

Overall, while interpretations may vary, the mark of the beast is generally understood as a symbol of allegiance to evil or participation in a system opposed to God, often associated with End Times scenarios and the fulfilment of biblical prophecy.

We need to know when the text about the mark of the beast would have been written. This is so that we can see which Anunnaki would have been in charge at that time. If you have read my chapter on who Yahweh was, you will know that the power changed hands around 3000 BCE.

The phrase *"mark of the beast"* specifically refers to a passage in the Book of Revelation in the New Testament of the Christian Bible. The Book of Revelation is believed to have been written by the Apostle John around 95–96 CE. It is the primary source for the concept of the mark of the beast in Christian theology.

However, similar themes of a mark or symbol associated with allegiance to a malevolent force or a repressive system can be found in other ancient texts, though not always explicitly referred to as the mark of the beast.

Here are a few examples:
The Book of Daniel: While the Book of Daniel does not mention the mark of the beast specifically, it contains themes of persecution and resistance against oppressive rulers.

In Daniel 7 and Daniel 11, there are references to a figure known as the *"Little Horn"* or *"King of Fierce Countenance"* who imposes his authority over the people and those who refuse to comply face persecution.

The Book of Ezekiel: Similar to Daniel, the Book of Ezekiel contains prophecies about oppressive rulers and the consequences of rebellion against them. While not explicitly mentioning a mark of the beast, it contains themes relevant to the broader concept of oppressive regimes and resistance.

Various apocalyptic texts: From the inter-testamental period, such as the Book of Enoch and the Apocalypse of Baruch, contain themes of cosmic conflict, divine judgment, and the persecution of the righteous by oppressive powers. These texts may provide background context for understanding the imagery and themes found in the Book of Revelation.

If you have seen my documentary on the Book of Revelation, you will know some of the events in the book are not talking about things to come, but actually things that had already happened. With this knowledge, when we look at the text about the mark of the beast, we can say that it is possible the mark of the beast has already happened.

Revelation chapter 13, verse 18.
In this passage, John tells us that the mark of the beast calculates to 666. The reason why six is a significant number is because it is commonly known as the number of man, whereas seven is known as the number of completion.

People were created on the sixth day, and on the seventh day, God rested and intended man to rest and to remember Him.
Of course that's not correct if you have read book 1.

If we look at the Anunnaki texts, they use 6 as their number 10; they counted in 6, we count in 10, they gave us the time, 60 seconds in a minute, 60 minutes in an hour, they gave us 360 degrees, and the first 6 humans failed, and the seventh was fine and we know that first Homo sapiens as Adamu (not Adam) so let us look back at what people think 666 means:

The reason why six is a significant number is because it is commonly known as the number of man, whereas seven is known as the number of completion.
That fits better than people were created on the sixth day, and on the seventh day rested, because the Anunnaki did not create Homo sapiens on the 6th day, it was about 144,000 years later.

There are obviously many, many different theories about what the mark of the beast could be, but now it is time to see what I can find out.

A God told his people to put his commandments on their hands and between their eyes or on their forehead as a sign.

Now, this instruction did not mean they were to literally strap his commandments to their head or hand. Rather, a God was using figurative language to tell them to obey his commandments with their actions, thinking, and will.

The Book of Revelation, which contains the passage about the mark of the beast, was written before any specific mention of the mark itself.

Revelation is traditionally attributed to the Apostle John and is the last book of the New Testament in the Christian Bible.

This means whoever wrote it was a Christian and, therefore, again, there is no evidence that the mark of the beast has anything to do with Christians, except for the author who copied older texts.

I will forget any version of the Bible except for Young's Literal Translation. I have proved all the other versions have changed.

"And I stood upon the sand of the sea, and I saw out of the sea a beast coming up, having seven heads and ten horns, and upon its horns ten diadems, and upon its heads a name of evil speaking.

And the beast that I saw was like to a leopard, and its feet as of a bear, and its mouth as the mouth of a lion. And the dragon did give to it his power and his throne and great authority. And I saw one of its heads as slain to death, and its deadly stroke was healed, and all the earth did wonder after the beast."

I can break this down: *"And I stood upon the sand of the sea, and I saw out of the sea a beast coming up, having seven heads and ten horns, and upon its horns ten diadems, and upon its heads a name of evil speaking."*

A dragon is a comet, but a comet can become a demon. If the comet entered Earth's atmosphere, then the Anunnaki called any meteors a demon, so a dragon is a comet with a long tail. (See my chapter on Demons.)

1. The Great Red Dragon (Revelation)
   Revelation (The Apocalypse of John), Chapter 12, Verse 3 (New Testament).

"Then another portent appeared in heaven: a great red dragon, with seven heads and ten horns, and seven diadems (Greek: διαδήματα, diadēmata) on his heads. His tail swept down a third of the stars of heaven and threw them to the earth."

Diadems are explicitly mentioned on its seven heads.

The Greeks called comets *'long-haired stars' (ἀστὴρ κομήτης);* the Babylonians saw them as *'celestial dragons.'"*
Comets in Ancient Cultures, NASA (2005)

"Comet 12P/Pons-Brooks is one of the brightest known periodic comets. It earned the nickname of 'devil comet' in 2023 when an outburst caused the comet to have an asymmetrical appearance, like having horns." NASA website.

Dragon Accounts from Ancient Texts:

Account 1: The 50-Biru Dragon
Source: Fragmentary Babylonian Creation text (possibly KAR 307), predating the Enuma Elish.
Description: A dragon slain by an unnamed deity, with blood flowing for 3 years, 3 months, 1 day, and 1 night. No horns, crown, or diadem described.
Size in Ancient Units:
  Length: 50 beru
  – Thickness: 1 beru
  – Mouth: 6 cubits (approximately 9 ft / 2.7 m) wide
  – Ears: 12 cubits (approximately 18 ft / 5.5 m) circumference

Size in Modern Units:
  – Length: 500–600 km (310–370 miles)
  – Thickness: 10–12 km (6.2–7.5 miles)

Account 2: The 60-Biru Dragon
Source: Fragmented Babylonian account (e.g., CT XIII 33-34).
Description: A dragon with no horns, crown, or diadem mentioned.

Size in Ancient Units:
- Length: 60 beru
- Thickness: 30 beru
- Eyes: 0.5 beru diameter each
- Paws: 20 beru long

Size in Modern Units:
- Length: 600–720 km (370–450 miles)
- Thickness: 300–360 km (185–225 miles)
- Eyes: 5–6 km (3.1–3.7 miles)
- Paws: 200–240 km (125–150 miles)

Were dragons real creatures 450 miles long in ancient times? That is huge, but if it was a comet then the tail could be that long.

In 1996, amateur astronomer Yuji Hyakutake made a remarkable discovery when he spotted what would come to be known as Comet Hyakutake, officially designated C/1996 B2. That same year, the comet made a very close approach to Earth, offering astronomers an extraordinary opportunity to study its features in detail.

One of its most astonishing characteristics was the length of its tail, stretching an incredible 570 million kilometres (about 354 million miles), which equates to roughly 3.8 astronomical units.

To put that into perspective, one astronomical unit is the average distance between the Earth and the Sun.

The tail was primarily composed of ionized gas, or plasma, made visible by interactions with the solar wind. This event marked the longest comet tail ever directly observed by scientists.

When it comes to the physical body of a comet, the nucleus, often described as a *"dirty snowball"* made of ice and rock, most are relatively small, typically only a few kilometres across.

For example, Halley's Comet has a nucleus about 15 kilometres long, while the well-studied Comet 67P/Churyumov–Gerasimenko, visited by the Rosetta spacecraft, is only about 4 kilometres wide.
However, there are exceptions. One such exception is Comet C/2002 VQ94 (LINEAR), discovered by the Lincoln Near-Earth Asteroid Research (LINEAR) project. Its nucleus is estimated to be approximately 96 kilometres (60 miles) in diameter, making it significantly larger than the average comet.

Due to the limits of observation at the time, this size estimate was based on brightness measurements and assumptions about the object's reflectivity, rather than direct imaging. Even more impressive is Comet C/2014 UN271, also known as Bernardinelli–Bernstein, which was first detected in 2014 but not confirmed as a comet until 2021.

Based on observations from the Hubble Space Telescope, scientists have estimated its nucleus to be between 100 and 150 kilometres (60 to 90 miles) across. As of 2022, it holds the title of the largest comet nucleus ever identified, marking a significant milestone in our understanding of these icy wanderers of the solar system.

When the comet entered Earth's atmosphere it became a fireball, just like a dragon breathing fire.

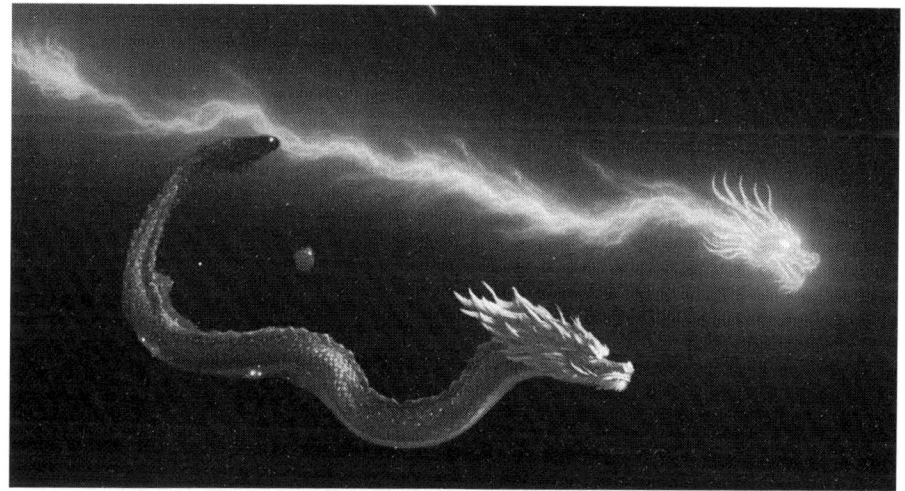

A comet with it's long tail and a Chinese dragon

Ever wonder why the Chinese dragon looks like a comet? Depicted as a long, serpentine being with a sinuous body, a prominent head, and a tail that can stretch across the sky. If you want to see more about dragons being comets, please look at the *"Dragon"* chapter.

This is a footnote from the book, Cuneiform Parallels to the Old Testament. Written in 1912, it is a book of translations of the ancient text that the Bible copied.

Plate number eight.

"Conflict between a God as the representative of cosmos and a horned dragon as the representative of chaos. In the early mythology, it was Enlil who thus destroyed the dragon. In the later mythology, it was Marduk who assumed this role, and when the Hebrews caught up with these mythological ideas, the role of destroyer was taken by Yahweh." L.W. King

In that book, there are three segments of translation that the author titled The Dragon and Demons, Aheil and the Labu, the legend of the seven evil demons. Remember this as I read the next part of the Book of Revelation about the mark of the beast.

"And the beast that I saw was like to a leopard, and its feet as of a bear, and its mouth as the mouth of a lion. And the dragon did give to it his power and his throne and great authority."

You will be thinking, what has a leopard got to do with dragons and demons? It is a good question.

Here is more translations from the same book, Cuneiform Parallels to the Old Testament.

"Raging storms. Evil Gods, are they ruthless demons who in Heaven's vault were created, are they? Workers of evil, are they? They lift up the head to evil, every day to evil. Of these seven, the first is the south wind. The second is a dragon whose mouth is opened that none can measure. The third is a grim leopard which carries off the young. The fourth is a terrible shibu. The fifth is a furious wolf who knoweth not to flee. The sixth is a rampant which marches against God and King. The seventh is a storm, an evil wind which takes vengeance. Seven are they, messengers of King Anu are they, from city to city darkness. Work they, a hurricane which mightily hunts in the heavens are they? Thick clouds that bring darkness in heaven."

We know space is heaven, so the demons were created in space.

We know the planet Tiamat was broken up, and the asteroid belt is the remains of the planet. We know this because of the Enuma Elish tablets in the British Museum.

Now you know that the dragon is a comet, a demon is a meteorite, and they named asteroids as leopard, shibu, and wolf, etc. They were all coming to Earth from heaven (space), so when they stood on the sand and could see the beast coming up, it was not from the ocean, it was from the curve of the Earth and coming towards them.

Now here is the full text from the Book of Revelation, and I hope you start to work out what it is really telling us. Yes, it even mentions a dragon when talking about the mark of the beast. I will explain more if you do not catch on to what Revelation is talking about.

Revelation 13, Young's Literal Translation.

"And I saw one of its heads as slain to death, and its deadly stroke was healed, and all the earth did wonder after the beast. And they did bow before the dragon who did give authority to the beast, and they did bow before the beast, saying, 'Who is like to the beast? Who is able to war with it?' And there was given to it a mouth speaking great things and evil speakings, and there was given to it authority to make war forty-two months.
And it did open its mouth for evil speaking toward God, to speak evil of His name and of His tabernacle and of those who in the heaven tabernacle. And there was given to it to make war with the saints and to overcome them, and there was given to it authority over every tribe and tongue and nation.

And bow before it shall all who are dwelling upon the land, whose names have not been written in the scroll of the life of the Lamb, slain from the foundation of the world.

If anyone hath an ear, let him hear. If anyone a captivity doth gather, into captivity he doth go away. If anyone by sword doth kill, it behoveth him by sword to be killed. Here is the endurance and the faith of the saints.

And I saw another beast coming up out of the land, and it had two horns, like a lamb, and it was speaking as a dragon. And all the authority of the first beast doth it do before it, and it maketh the land and those dwelling in it that they shall bow before the first beast, whose deadly stroke was healed. And it doth great signs, that fire also it may make to come down from the heaven to the earth before men.

And it leadeth astray those dwelling on the land, because of the signs that were given it to do before the beast, saying to those dwelling upon the land, to make an image to the beast that hath the stroke of the sword, and did live. And there was given to it to give a spirit to the image of the beast, that also the image of the beast may speak, and that it may cause as many as shall not bow before the image of the beast, that they may be killed.

And it maketh all, the small and the great, and the rich, and the poor, and the freemen, and the servants, that it may give to them a mark upon their right hand or upon their foreheads. And that no one may be able to buy, or to sell, except he who is having the mark, or the name of the beast, or the number of his name. Here is the wisdom. He who is having the understanding, let him count the number of the beast, for the number of a man it is, and its number is 666."

It seems to me that the Anunnaki warned people about the asteroids and meteors (Dragons and Leopards) and that it was a time where someone, one of the Anunnaki, took advantage of the destruction. I am not talking about one or two meteors, I am talking about loads that would have come down in smaller fragments.

Comets = Dragons
Demon – Meteorite
Leopard = Asteroid
Vipers = Group of smaller asteroids

If you think it is strange that the mark of the beast text is talking about comets and meteors as living creatures, then I can show you that in the ancient texts that predate the Bible called the Enuma Elish, the Anunnaki talked about planets as living creatures, just like the mark of the beast talked about the beast being alive.

Here is part of the Enuma Elish, where Tiamat, which is a planet, is getting attacked by other smaller planets:

"They are furious, they devise mischief without resting night and day, they prepare for battle, fuming and raging, they have joined their forces and are making war. They have made them of lofty stature, whoever beholdeth them is overcome by terror, their bodies rear up, and none can withstand their attack.
She has set up vipers and dragons and the monster Lahamu (Venus) and hurricanes and raging hounds and scorpion men and mighty tempests and fishmen and rams. They bear cruel weapons, without fear of the fight, her commands are mighty, none can resist them.

After this fashion, huge of stature, hath she made eleven monsters. (Rocks from the planet) Among the Gods who are her sons, inasmuch as he hath given her support, she hath exalted king. In their midst she hath raised him to power, to march before the forces, to lead the host, to give the battle signal, to advance to the attack."

The large ones that are mentioned are the ones that caused the most destruction, that is why they said this:

"That fire also it may make to come down from the heaven to the earth before men."

So my conclusion is:

One of the Anunnaki Gods knew a comet (Dragon) was heading towards Earth and told humans from another land that if they want to live they would have to follow him, change their allegiance to his by marking their hand or wearing a bandanna on their head with his name.

The ones that did not follow that God (Anunnaki) got killed by the beast when it came into Earth's atmosphere and hit the ground.

Chapter 8

Who Was Jesus' Father?

Who was Jesus, and who was his dad? I am approaching this from the premise that there is no almighty being as thought of in the Bible.

Who would have been around at the time to be Jesus' dad? Would this figure have had the power to take Mary up to space, referred to as *"heaven"* in the texts?

If he was a God (Anunnaki) that created Jesus, were there other Gods present, given the concept of monotheism and Jesus' teachings about one true God?
Had this figure done something like this before, attempting to establish himself as the sole God? And if other Gods were around, why were not they Jesus' father?

To understand Jesus' identity, we must turn to the Bible, as no Anunnaki or Sumerian texts mention him. This absence is expected, given that the Sumerian language gradually declined as a spoken language and was replaced by Akkadian and others, continued in written form only until the end of the third millennium BCE. After that point, Sumerian texts became increasingly rare, and later records were written in other languages.

Since the third millennium BCE predates the birth of Jesus by over two thousand years, he is believed to have been born around 4–6 BCE, there is no historical overlap between Jesus and the period when Sumerian texts were actively produced.

So, who would have been around at that time to be his dad? The Anunnaki, whose race name is Dingir, translates to *"Gods,"* were here and originated from a planet called Nibiru.

They were called Gods, and rightly so, just as we have *"human"* or *"humans."* They also referred to themselves as lords, with the great lord being Enki (Enki and Ninmah : c.1.1.2) who created Homo sapiens.

You might know him as *"our father who art in heaven."* But, as shown, heaven is space, indicating Enki came from there.

You might think Enki was Jesus' dad. No. The original Gods like Enlil, Enki, and Ninmah would have either been way too old or had died long before Jesus' time.
We can see this when Gilgamesh talks about the Gods of old, meaning they are not around anymore.

The Epic of Gilgamesh speaks of the Gods of old, recounting a time when they caused the flood: "

The Gods were frightened by the flood and retreated, ascending to the heaven of Anu. The Gods were cowering like dogs, crouching by the outer wall. Ishtar shrieked like a woman in childbirth, the sweet-voiced mistress of the Gods wailed. '
The olden days have alas turned to clay because I said evil things in the assembly of the Gods. How could I say evil things in the assembly of the Gods, ordering a catastrophe to destroy my people?

No sooner have I given birth to my dear people than they fill the sea like so many fish.'

The Gods, those of the Anunnaki, were weeping with her, humbly sitting, sobbing with grief, their lips burning, parched with thirst. Six days and seven nights came the wind and flood, the storm flattening the land."

Marduk, Enki's son, is the hero in the Enuma Elish tablets housed in the British Museum, where he is described as destroying the planet Tiamat. However, Marduk was not born at that time, as part of Tiamat's destruction formed Earth.

My calculations suggest the Enuma Elish was written about 5,000–6,000 years ago, (3-4,000 BC) around the time some believe Earth was formed, though it is more likely when the story of Marduk spread as a creation narrative.

Marduk was banished at one point and chased out of Babylon by Enlil and his granddaughter Inanna (also known as Ishtar).

For context, Enlil was the first main God, the wrathful God in the Bible.
Ninurta, Enlil's son, was next in line to succeed him. Although Enlil's half-brother Enki was born first, he was born to a concubine, not the king Anu's wife, making Enlil's lineage through the king's wife primary and he Ninurta would also have the option to take over from King Anu on their home planet or take over from his father Enlil on Earth, but logically he would have gone back home to Nibiru.

Thus, Ninurta would not typically become Earth's ruler. However, because the Anunnaki aged faster on Earth, Enki and Enlil and their sister Ninmah likely died here on Earth. King Anu would have needed Ninurta to return to Nibiru to eventually take over.

Enlil and Ninurta allowed Marduk to lead Earth; this was mainly because Enlil allowed Ninurta to use *"weapons of terror"* to destroy the cities that people were helping Marduk; you will know that story from the Bible in the Book of Revelation.

One of the seven weapons was a nuke bomb which gave off radiation but the wind changed and all the lands that Enlil and Ninurta had were wiped out; you will know the passage in the Bible Zechariah 14:12 (NIV):
"This is the plague with which the Lord will strike all the nations that have fought against Jerusalem: their flesh will rot while they stand on their feet, their eyes will rot in their sockets, and their tongues will rot in their mouths."

What tablet before the Bible says anything like that? It is called the Epic of Erra (Erra was Nergal, another son of Enki).
The Epic of Erra (Tablet IV, lines 40–45, approximate translation)
The God Erra (or his plague-demons, the Sebitti) is described as wreaking havoc:
"The warrior Erra will strike them down, their flesh will dissolve... He who is struck by [Erra's] weapons—his flesh is dissolved as if by the samasnu-disease."

There is more to those tablets; it is about a 30 minute read.

Because the wind changed, Marduk's people were saved from the radiation and it was only them left; this left Enlil no choice but to allow Marduk to become the most high.

I will recap what we have gone through.

Question 1: Who would be around at that time to be his dad?
Answer: Anunnaki, race name Gods.

Question 2: Would the dad have the power to take Mary up to heaven?

Erich von Däniken's 1968 book Chariots of the Gods was among the first to suggest aliens influenced our past. The word *"chariot"* typically implies something horse-drawn, as used in ancient times.

However, like *"vehicle,"* it can have broader meanings: a car, truck, or even a spacecraft. Could a chariot be a spacecraft going into heaven, meaning space?

Ancient texts suggest the Anunnaki did fly.

For example:

The tablet **The Return of Ninurta to Nibru**, a turgida to Ninurta, C1, 6.1:

"Let my father therefore bring in my battle trophies and weapons for me. Let Enlil bathe my heroic arms. Let him pour holy water on the fierce arms which bore my weapons. Let him set up a holy dais in the throne room.

Let him set my heavenly chariot upon a pedestal. Let him tether my captured warriors there like budding bulls. Let him have my captured kings make obeisance to me there as to the light of heaven."

Why call his chariot *"heavenly"*? I have never called my car heavenly.

There are descriptions of their crafts, one called a *"whirlwind."* Zecharia Sitchin describes it as a one- or two-person helicopter.

The Bible mentions something similar in **2 Kings 2:1–12** (King James Version):

"And it came to pass, when the Lord would take up Elijah into heaven by a whirlwind, that Elijah went with Elisha from Gilgal... And it came to pass, as they still went on and talked, that, behold, there appeared a chariot of fire, and horses of fire, and parted them both asunder; and Elijah went up by a whirlwind into heaven."

The whirlwind is mentioned twelve times in this passage. There is a strong possibility this flying machine was carved in Egypt, above a door in Abydos, depicting futuristic machines.

Whirlwind

OUR TRUE HISTORY

Heavenly chariot

These are what my research leads me to believe they are.

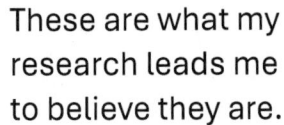
Solar boat / barque

Ninurta's Blackbird

Another Sumerian text describes hovering:

" *Lugalbanda in the Mountain Cave, C1.8.2.1, a second time.*

That is, at the following sunrise, as the bright bull rising up from the horizon. The bull resting among the cypress is a shield standing on the ground watched by the assembly, a shield coming out from the treasury watched by the young men.

The youth Utu extended his holy splendor down from heaven... His good protective God hovered ahead of him. His good protective Goddess walked behind him. The God which had smitten him stepped aside... When he raised his eyes heavenward to Utu, he wept to him as to his own father."

The Anunnaki used large machines to move gold to Mars, where the Igigi, meaning *"eyes in the sky,"* the watchers resided.

Question 2: Would the father of Jesus have the power to take Mary up to heaven?
Answer: Anunnaki, race name Gods, in their chariots.

Question 3: If he is a God, were there other Gods because of monotheism?
The Bible portrays Jesus within a monotheistic framework, emphasising belief in one God. Christianity, based on Jesus' teachings, adheres to this.

In the New Testament, Jesus affirms this, often referring to God as *"father"* and teaching the unity of God. For example, in: **Mark 12:29**, Jesus says, *"The most important one is this: Hear, O Israel, the Lord our God, the Lord is one."*
The Gospel of John reinforces this monotheistic belief while emphasising Jesus' connection to God.

So why would Jesus' father want Jesus to proclaim one God when the Anunnaki are many and their race name is Gods, were many?

Enuma Elish, Tablet VI: Given Marduk full control of Earth.

"We give thee sovereignty over the whole world. Sit thou down in might; be exalted in thy command. Thy weapon shall never lose its power; it shall crush thy foe."

Although Enki, *"our father who art in heaven,"* created Homo sapiens, Jesus' dad was not Enki.
I believe Marduk was Jesus' father, the ruler of Earth from around 3000 BCE.

Question 4: Did the dad do this before?
Marduk was once in charge of ancient Egypt as Ra, later Amun-Ra after the flood, representing the next God in the Egyptian Ogdoad, meaning *"hidden of name, heaven, or sun."*
As the sun God Ra, his father was Ptah (Enki).
Ptah is credited with creating animals and humans on the potter's wheel of Khnum (clay again) but only one could have created humans and the hybrid creatures.

Later, Marduk became Aten, another sun God. He left Egypt when Enlil and Inanna pursued him but returned after other pharaohs shifted worship to other Gods.

Marduk reinserted his own pharaohs, enlisting his father's help I believe to create a new human type fused with grey alien DNA. (Greys are the modern type of small alien we hear about with the big almond-shaped black eyes).

Because of stories from the Native Americans and ancient wall art it seems the greys (or a species like them with elongated heads) visited Earth in our near distant past.

Watch my documentary on Elongated Skulls to see that there were natural and head bound ones.
(Fake image for copyright reasons)

Ancient Carvings/Wall Art Resembling Grey Aliens:

- **Charama, India:** Cave paintings of humanoids with round heads, no facial features, in suits, with disc-shaped objects. ~10,000 years old. Found by JR Bhagat, 2014.
- **Sego Canyon, Utah, USA:** Petroglyphs of life-sized figures with hollow eyes, no arms/legs. ~8,000 years old. Anasazi/Fremont/Ute tribes.
- **Toro Muerto, Peru:** Petroglyphs of humanoid figures with elongated heads. Prehistoric.
- **Val Camonica,** Italy: Petroglyphs of suited humanoids with strange objects. ~10,000 BCE. Found by Walter Laeng, 1909.

- **Tassili n'Ajjer, Algeria:** Rock art of stick-like figures in helmets, with aerial objects. ~7,000–10,000 years old.
- **Kimberley, Australia (Wandjina):** Paintings of tall figures with greyish eyes, triangular heads. ~5,000 years old. Noted by George Grey, 1838.
- **Barrier Canyon, Utah, USA:** Pictographs of elongated figures with bug-like eyes, no arms/legs. ~9,000 years old. Documented by David Sucec/Craig Law.

Whistleblowers tell us grey aliens have set up bases in caves. But was there another race?

The Hopi tribes speak of the Ant people, really small space people. In September 2023, Mexican journalist and UFO enthusiast Jaime Maussan presented two small, mummified bodies to Mexico's Congress, claiming they were non-human entities over 1,000 years old. The specimens, reportedly discovered in Peru, featured elongated skulls and three-fingered hands.

These have not been debunked, even though people will tell you they have; in fact the more research done on them the more real they are proving to be.

There is a document called SOM 101 special operations manual, which many believe to be real and is a manual from the 1950s for the military on how to handle a crashed UFO; in the pages it talks about two types of aliens, EBE 1 and EBE 2 (Extraterrestrial Biological Entity) and they both had elongated skulls; could any of the aliens' DNA been used to create the bloodline of a new ruler in Egypt?

- **Thutmose IV** – The skeleton has elongated skull.
  └─ **Amenhotep III** – The skeleton does not appear to have elongated skull, however his wife Queen Tiye does appear to have a longer skull.

└─ **Akhenaten** – KV55 is a tomb in the Valley of the Kings that contained a mummy with an elongated skull, likely belonging to a male of the Amarna period—possibly **Akhenaten** or a close relative.
  └─ **Tutankhamun** – Mummy in British Museum does show elongated skull.

There are differences in the types of headbound skulls found:
Headbound elongated skull:
- Result of deliberate cranial binding or shaping during infancy.
- Sutures remain intact but skull is stretched or compressed.
- Shape is symmetrical and controlled.

Elongated skull with missing suture:
- Natural skull elongation.
- Sutures missing.
- Thicker bone in the skull.
- The foramen magnum is further back.
- Larger brain capacity.
- Seem to mostly have red hair.

Could Marduk have created a human with an elongated head like the greys? If you look at the body proportions of Akhenaten some people could say yes!
That would mean Akhenaten was not fully Homo sapiens, possibly with big hips and an elongated skull!

A hybrid became Pharaoh Artutama I I believe was created to maintain the pharaoh line true to Aten (Marduk); he created a female, leading to a lineage including Akhenaten, Queen Nefertiti, and Tutankhamun, all with elongated skulls.

Marduk, as Aten, enforced monotheistic worship of himself.

Question 4: Did the dad do this before?
Answer: Yes, Marduk did, son of Enki.

Question 5: If there were other Gods around, why were not they the father of Jesus?

If Marduk had red hair and used his DNA for the pharaohs this would explain why elongated skulls, even outside Egypt, often have red hair. Ancient texts describe Enki and Enlil with blonde hair and blue eyes, but some Anunnaki may have had red hair, explaining the red-haired Nephilim, offspring of Anunnaki-human mating.

Why Marduk? As Jesus' father, Marduk likely instructed him to promote monotheism, as he changed the many Gods to just one God; we can see the many Gods with Genesis 1:26's plural *"Let us make man in our image,"* indicating multiple Gods.

Why doesn't the Bible talk about the Gods more if there were many?
The Bible's words were altered to favour one God over an alien race for population control.
In the original Hebrew Bible, the plural form *"gods"* (אֱלֹהִם - Elohim) appears approximately 2,570 times.
In most modern English Bible translations, the word *"gods"* appears about 200 to 300 times, depending on the version.

If Jesus was a hybrid and the son of an alien this could also explain Jesus' miracles, enabled by his father's advanced technology for healing, destruction, and God (Marduk) appearing as a star in Bethlehem's sky.
To me it's clear Marduk created Jesus.

Chapter 9

Why Was Jesus Born?

Reflecting on the previous chapter, where I suggested Marduk created Jesus because he had already crafted hybrids and placed them in charge in Egypt, a pressing question emerges: why create Jesus?

Unlike those earlier hybrids, he held no dominion, ruling neither a country nor the planet.

Could it be that Marduk made him merely for amusement? By *"made,"* I mean genetically created, not born through the union of a male and female, a virgin birth!

In this chapter, I will explore the reasons behind Jesus' birth and shed light on why I believe Marduk permitted his death.

Let us start with the mainstream perspective.

The prevailing belief is that Jesus was born around 4–6 BCE in Bethlehem, a conclusion drawn from the Gospels of Matthew and Luke, supported by historical and theological analysis.

These accounts, including Matthew 1:18–25 and Luke 2:1–7, depict his virgin birth to Mary through divine intervention by the Holy Spirit during Herod the Great's reign, which ended in 4 BCE.
The mention of a census under Quirinius (Luke 2:2) aligns with Roman records, though exact dates are debated, placing the birth before 4 BCE.

Theologically, Christians view this as fulfilling Old Testament prophecies, such as Isaiah 7:14, marking Jesus as the incarnation of God's son sent to redeem humanity, a celebration known as Christmas.

This consensus relies on scriptural interpretation and limited historical corroboration, with scholars adjusting for timeline discrepancies. The first two points merely outline a timeline of events; it is the last one, Jesus' birth as the fulfilment of Old Testament prophecies that warrants closer examination.

At first glance, without historical knowledge, one might assume, as I did, that Jesus was placed on Earth as a special figure to fulfil prophecies. However, history reveals a different picture: there were numerous prophets before him, around 24 to 26 individuals capable of delivering prophecies. Yet, Jesus is portrayed not as a prophet making new predictions but as one fulfilling existing ones.

The Hebrew Bible records the words of many prophets, and Christianity identifies several, such as Isaiah, Jeremiah, Daniel, Micah, Zechariah, Malachi, Hosea, Joel, and David (whose psalms are seen as prophetic) as having delivered prophecies fulfilled by Jesus, thus supporting Christian claims of his role as the Messiah.

In contrast, Jewish tradition does not view these prophecies as fulfilled in Jesus, often interpreting them as referring to historical events or a future Messiah yet to come.

Other prophets' messages were either fulfilled in different historical contexts or remain debated among scholars and theologians.

Some Christians argue that the prophecies Jesus fulfilled were so remarkable that only a divine figure could achieve them, pointing to his unique identity as the Son of God. This raises a question: what set Jesus apart? Consider the *"sons of God"* in Genesis 6:1–4, often interpreted as angelic beings who fathered children with human women, producing the Nephilim.

The sons of God were the Igigi; these were real Gods, not hybrids.

Let us examine the prophecies Jesus himself made and their outcomes, noting that much depends on translation and belief. I will share my thoughts on each fulfilled prophecy:

1. His Own Death and Resurrection: Jesus predicted in Matthew 16:21, Mark 8:31, Luke 9:22, and John 2:19–21 that the Son of Man would suffer, be killed, and rise on the third day.

The Gospels record his crucifixion and resurrection within three days (Matthew 27, 28; Mark 15, 16; Luke 23, 24; John 19, 20), central to Christian faith and considered historically fulfilled by the early church.

My thoughts: Critics, including some biblical scholars like the Jesus Seminar, argue these prophecies could have been written retrospectively to match the events. The Gospels were composed decades after the events, during a time when the early church was shaping its narrative.

The detailed alignment of Jesus' death and resurrection with his predictions (e.g., *"on the third day"*) might reflect theological shaping after the fact, especially since Mark's account, the earliest, lacks post-resurrection details, suggesting later embellishment in Matthew, Luke, and John.

My own counterargument: The presence of the prediction in multiple independent sources (Mark, Q material in Matthew/Luke, John) and its early attestation in Paul's letters (1 Corinthians 15:3–4, c. 55 CE, pre-dating the Gospels) suggest it was part of the oral tradition before the crucifixion.

The awkward phrasing (e.g., John 2:19 misinterpreted by listeners as the Temple) and the disciples' initial disbelief (Luke 24:11) argue against a fabricated prophecy, as these details would be unlikely if invented post-event.

My concern: The problem here is that right now, in this book, I can write that the Titanic will sink; if I do not put a date on this book, someone reading it in the future, 2,000 years later, might think the book was written before the Titanic sank and thus I can see the future.

2. **Betrayal by a Close Associate:** In Matthew 26:21–25, Mark 14:18–21, and John 13:21–26, Jesus foretold betrayal by one of the Twelve, fulfilled by Judas Iscariot (Matthew 26:47–50, John 18:2–5).
3.

My thoughts: The prediction appears across all four Gospels with variations, suggesting a shared oral tradition. The specific identification of *"one of the Twelve"* (e.g., John 13:26 naming Judas) and the fulfilment in Judas handing Jesus over to the authorities align closely, supporting its authenticity.

Paul's reference to Jesus' betrayal in 1 Corinthians 11:23 (c. 55 CE) predates the Gospels, indicating the event was part of the early Christian narrative, potentially tracing back to Jesus' lifetime.

However, the Gospels were written 30–70 years after the crucifixion (Mark c. 65–70 CE, Matthew and Luke c. 80–90 CE, John c. 90–110 CE), allowing for retrospective shaping. The detailed prediction might have been crafted after Judas' betrayal to fit the narrative of Jesus' foreknowledge. The betrayal story enhances the messianic portrayal (e.g., fulfilling Psalm 41:9, *"Even my close friend, whom I trusted... has lifted up his heel against me"*), suggesting theological embellishment post-event.

3. Denial by Peter: Jesus predicted in Matthew 26:34, Luke 22:34, and John 13:38 that Peter would deny him three times before the rooster crowed, fulfilled during the trial (Matthew 26:69–75, John 18:15–27).

My thoughts: The prediction appears across multiple Gospels with slight variations (e.g., *"before the rooster crows"* in Matthew and Luke, *"before you hear the rooster crow"* in John), and the fulfilment is detailed consistently, with Peter denying Jesus three times during his trial, followed by a rooster crowing (Matthew 26:74–75, John 18:27). The event is part of the Passion narrative, reflected in early Christian creeds and Paul's letters (e.g., 1 Corinthians 15:3–5), suggesting it was established in oral tradition shortly after Jesus' death (c. 30–33 CE).

4. Scattering of the Disciples: Citing Zechariah 13:7 in Matthew 26:31 and Mark 14:27, Jesus foresaw the disciples deserting him, fulfilled when they fled at his arrest (Matthew 26:56, Mark 14:50).

My thoughts: The fulfilment of Jesus' prophecy about the scattering of the disciples is widely accepted in Christian theology as evidence of his foreknowledge, supported by the Zechariah 13:7 allusion and Gospel accounts.

However, it can be debated due to the potential for retrospective writing (given the 30–70-year gap), textual adaptations, lack of external evidence, and the plausibility of the prediction.

5. Destruction of the Temple: In Matthew 24:1–2, Mark 13:1–2, and Luke 21:5–6, Jesus predicted the Temple's destruction, fulfilled in 70 CE by the Romans (Josephus, Jewish Wars).

My thoughts: The Gospels were written after 70 CE (Mark c. 65–70 CE, just before or during the event; Matthew and Luke c. 80–90 CE, post-destruction), raising the possibility of retrospective writing. The prophecy might have been crafted or emphasised after the event to validate Jesus' foreknowledge.

I will not add my thoughts on the prophecies he did not complete. The unfulfilled or eschatological prophecies include:

Second Coming and End of the Age (Matthew 24:29–31, Mark 13:24–27, Luke 21:25–28), which remains unfulfilled after over 2,000 years, interpreted as a delayed return or future event (e.g., Revelation 19–22).

The Great Tribulation and Abomination of Desolation (Matthew 24:15–21, Mark 13:14–19), partially fulfilled with the 70 CE siege but awaiting a full tribulation.

The Gospel Preached to All Nations (Matthew 24:14, Mark 13:10), unfulfilled as not every nation is reached.

Restoration of Israel (Luke 21:24), partially fulfilled with 1948 but awaiting complete restoration.

So far, nothing in these prophecies seems to justify Marduk creating Jesus.

However, a prophecy from someone else, uncompleted during Jesus' life, might explain his creation. I have mentioned that Marduk placed the Akhenaten bloodline in power in Egypt suddenly to rule.

What if he aimed to do the same in Israel?

First, let us consider where Marduk was around Jesus' time. We know he governed many places over his time on Earth, such as Babylon, Egypt, and even Mars at one point, but where was he when he created Jesus?
At that point, Marduk had transformed everything to worship just one God... himself, the one true God, as you may know him, the God of Israel.

Marduk took over from Enlil and was in Israel, but he faced trouble there as the Romans began to take over.

Roman General Pompey conquers Jerusalem 63 BCE 2,087 years ago, smack bang right around the time Jesus was born.

Marduk needed a king to fight on his behalf while he could then address the problem in Rome, where the Enlil family pantheon were.
The Pantheon, Rome: The original building was commissioned by Marcus Vipsanius Agrippa between **25–27 BCE** (approximately 2,050 years ago) during the reign of Augustus. Smack bang when Marduk's people was getting attacked in Israel.

So did Marduk create Jesus to be the king of Israel?

There are Old Testament prophecies about a future king or Messiah from Bethlehem.

These include **Micah 5:2,** which states, *"But you, Bethlehem Ephrathah, though you are small among the clans of Judah, out of you will come for me one who will be ruler over Israel, whose origins are from of old, from ancient times,"*

With **Matthew 2:1**, 5–6 affirming Jesus' birth in Bethlehem as the Messiah and ruler, linked to the Davidic line; **Zechariah 9:9**, *"Rejoice greatly, Daughter Zion! Shout, Daughter Jerusalem! See, your king comes to you, righteous and victorious, lowly and riding on a donkey, on a colt, the foal of a donkey,"* cited in John 12:14–15 and Matthew 21:1–5 during his triumphal entry, portraying him as the humble king.

Isaiah 9:6–7, *"For to us a child is born, to us a son is given, and the government will be on his shoulders... He will reign on David's throne and over his kingdom,"* connected to Jesus' birth in **Luke 1:32–33** and **Luke 2:11–14** as an eternal Davidic king.

Isaiah 11:1–2, *"A shoot will come up from the stump of Jesse; from his roots a Branch will bear fruit,"* linked to Jesus as the *"root of Jesse"* in **Romans 15:12** and **Revelation 22:16.**

Jeremiah 23:5–6, *"The days are coming... when I will raise up for David a righteous Branch, a King who will reign wisely,"* applied to Jesus in **Luke 1:32–33** and **Hebrews 1:8.**

At the time Marduk created Jesus, Enlil's family, his uncle's kin, were in Rome, controlling the pantheon, with worshippers known as Catholics.

Marduk tried to install this new hybrid son Jesus as king, possibly endowed with a superior brain due to mixing with an alien with an elongated head, like the Akhenaten bloodline.

See my videos on King Midas and Anunnaki in the Americas to see that the elongated skull people were smarter than the rest: www.ourtruehistory.co.uk

But here is where the problem began for Marduk: Jesus refused to be a king.

Several instances in the biblical accounts show where Jesus could have been proclaimed or perceived as a worldly king, yet he either explicitly refused or redefined his kingship.

During the Temptation in the Wilderness (**Matthew 4:8–10, Luke 4:5–8**), Satan offered him *"all the kingdoms of the world and their glory"* if he would bow down, but Jesus rejected it, stating worship is due to God alone.

After feeding the five thousand (**John 6:15**), the crowd intended to make him king by force, yet he withdrew to a mountain.

During his trial before Pilate (John 18:36–37), when asked if he was *"King of the Jews,"* Jesus clarified, *"My kingdom is not of this world... my kingdom is from another place,"* affirming a not fully human.

The Triumphal Entry into Jerusalem (**Matthew 21:1–11, Mark 11:1–11, Luke 19:28–44, John 12:12–19**) saw crowds hailing him as *"Son of David"* with cloaks and palm branches, but he entered humbly on a donkey, fulfilling **Zechariah 9:9**'s prophecy of a humble king, not a conquering leader.

Based on the New Testament, Jesus advocated for peace and non-violence rather than combat. He taught his followers to be *"peacemakers"* (**Matthew 5:9**), to *"turn the other cheek"* (Matthew 5:39), and to *"love your enemies and pray for those who persecute you"* (**Matthew 5:44**), rejecting retaliation.

During his arrest, when Peter drew a sword, Jesus said, *"Put your sword back in its place, for all who draw the sword will die by the sword"* (**Matthew 26:52**), and noted his kingdom was *"not of this world"* (**John 18:36**).

His non-violence was active resistance to dictatorship through peaceful means, not passive inaction, though **Matthew 10:34** (*"I did not come to bring peace, but a sword"*) is seen as a metaphor for division, not literal violence.

The Temple cleansing (**John 2:15**), where he drove out money changers, is interpreted as a symbolic act against corruption, not personal violence.

Clearly, Jesus knew who his father was, but he was a disappointment to Marduk, who left him to die.

On the cross, Jesus cried out, *"My God, my God, why have you forsaken me?"* (**Matthew 27:46; Mark 15:34**).

Some claim Jesus was born for our sins, citing **Romans 5:8**, *"But God demonstrates his own love for us in this: While we were still sinners, Christ died for us,"* written 23–28 years after his death (c. 53–58 CE), which a court would call hearsay.

The New Testament accounts, written by his followers after the events, not contemporaneously with his crucifixion, are prone to embellishment over time.

Consider Lucifer, whose backstory has grown from a single passage (e.g., **Isaiah 14:12**) suggesting his death, yet people add narratives claiming he is still alive and they give him a huge backstory for no reason.

After Jesus' death, Marduk travelled to Rome in his spacecraft. From Jesus' birth (6–4 BCE) to St. Peter's papacy (30–67 CE): ~35–71 years.
Later he instructed Constantine to build a temple for him, The Vatican, directing that people should not worship Enlil's family (the Roman pantheon) but only him, and those people became known as Christians.

To sum up my thoughts, Jesus was a hybrid, offered Israel to rule but turned it down, leading Marduk to turn his back on him and let him die.

Chapter 10

Demons

Far too many people label anything they dislike as a demon or even things they do not understand as a demon regardless of whether it fits the term. I have heard claims that aliens, djinn, elites, fallen angels, politicians, cryptids, and even video games are demons.

This overuse stems from a lack of understanding about what *"demon"* originally meant. Many point to the Bible as the source of demons, claiming false Gods were demons, but this is misguided when older texts, which the Bible drew from, provide clearer insight.

The Bible has been altered numerous times; consider how *"Lucifer,"* called the *"son of the morning star"* in the Hebrew Bible, KJV, became a proper name in the Latin Vulgate. Relying on modern interpretations without examining original sources is like saying a dog is a cat; repeat it enough, and some might believe it.

To understand *"demon,"* we must trace it to its earliest use. Some, with minimal research, claim the word comes from the Greek *"daimon"* (δαίμων), which referred to a neutral or even positive spirit, divine power, or guiding entity in ancient Greek culture, not inherently evil. However, this is only half the story.

The Greeks borrowed the concept from the Sumerians, who got it from the Anunnaki, the race called Gods who created humans.

The Sumerians used *"demon"* long before the Babylonians, a civilisation thriving at least 1,300–1,400 years before classical Greece.

A Babylonian carving of a "monster and demon" predates Greek usage, showing the term's deeper roots.

Berosus, a priest of Bel-Marduk (Lord Marduk) in Babylon, described monstrous beings from a time of darkness and watery abyss, created with hybrid forms:

"There appeared men, some with two wings, others with four, and with two faces... one body but two heads; the one that of a man, the other of a woman... Other human figures were to be seen with the legs and horns of goats...

Bulls with the heads of men, and dogs with fourfold bodies, terminated in their extremities with the tails of fishes... In short, there were creatures in which were combined the limbs of every species of animals."

These descriptions align with Enki's creation of hybrid creatures, as I have discussed in other chapters. The modern idea of demons as evil entities has been ingrained, but I propose a different origin: demons were initially space rocks, meteorites, not comets (which were called Dragons).

Translators of ancient texts, like those in the British Museum's The Babylonian Legends of the Creation, misinterpreted these meteorites as *"beings"* because they did not grasp the Anunnaki's terminology.

In **The Seven Tablets of Creation**, the authors describe the beginning:

"In the beginning nothing whatever existed except APSÛ, a boundless, confused and disordered mass of watery matter...

Out of this mass there were evolved two orders of beings, namely, demons and Gods. The demons had hideous forms... part animal, part bird, part reptile and part human. The Gods had wholly human forms, and they represented the three layers of the comprehensible world, that is to say, heaven or the sky, the atmosphere, and the underworld."

This interpretation assumes demons were creatures, but the Anunnaki called planets *"deities"* assigning them personalities and emotions. For example, in **The Story of Creation :**
"When above the heaven was not named, And beneath the earth bore no name, And the primeval Apsu, who begat them And Mummu and Tiamat, the mother of them all... Then were created the Gods in the midst of [heaven], Lakhmu and Lakhamu were called into being..."

Lakhmu (Mars) and Lakhamu (Venus) were planets, not beings, as confirmed by translations like Ryan Moorhen's from Columbia University tablets.

The Enuma Elish describes Tiamat, a massive ice planet, with emotions and speech:
"Apsu... cried unto Mummu... 'O Mummu... Come, unto Tiamat let us go!'... When Tiamat heard these words, She raged and cried aloud... She uttered a curse..."

Planets do not speak, but the Anunnaki personified them, much like we might call a car *"she."* The British Museum's Babylonian Legends of the Creation clarifies:
"The Gods are deifications of the sun, moon, planets and other stars, and APSÛ, or CHAOS, and his companions the demons, are personifications of darkness, night and evil."

Demons, then, were not planets but destructive space rocks, meteorites.

The Cuneiform Parallels to the Old Testament, translated by Robert William Rogers, describes these in The Legend of the Seven Evil Demons :
"Raging storms, evil Gods are they, Ruthless demons, who in heaven's vault were created... Workers of evil are they... They lift up the head to evil, every day to evil, Destruction to work."

Here, *"vault"* refers to the asteroid belt between Jupiter and Mars (see my chapter Firmament). *"Evil Gods"* are not full planets but massive rocks, possibly planet-sized, without stable orbits. Remember we have called Deities Gods! When really Deities were **celestial** bodies.

The text continues:
"Of these seven the first is the South wind... The second is a dragon, whose mouth is opened... The third is a grim leopard... The fourth is a terrible Shibbu... The fifth is a furious Wolf... The sixth is a rampant... which marches against God and king. The seventh is a storm, an evil wind, which takes vengeance."

Reworded for clarity, these are space rocks causing destruction:
Raging storms, space rocks in the asteroid belt, created to wreak havoc.
The first is the South wind; the second, a dragon (a comet with a tail, see my chapter Dragons); the third, a grim leopard (asteroid); the fourth, a terrible Shibbu; the fifth, a furious Wolf; the sixth, a rampant force; the seventh, a storm, an evil wind.

They are messengers of King Anu, ruler of space, flying from city to city, bringing darkness.
Like hurricanes hunting in space, they block the sun with thick clouds, flashing like lightning. Entering the atmosphere.

Enlil, hearing of these rocks storming the asteroid belt, consulted Ea (Enki). Sin (the moon), Shamash, and Ishtar were tasked with ordering the belt, but the rocks darkened the moon, prompting Enlil to send Nusku to warn Ea in the ocean.

These *"evil Gods (**celestial** bodies.)"* are huge asteroids, becoming meteorites when entering Earth's atmosphere, causing destruction. Over time, the human Sumerians repurposed *"demon"* to mean anything evil, not just space rocks.

For example, in Enki and Ninmah, a condition causing uncontrollable urination is attributed to a *"namtar demon"* (disease), not a literal entity.

In Dumuzid's Dream, *"demons"* are thugs or bad people setting fires and causing chaos.

The Sumerians named various evils as demons:
- Lamashtu: Blamed for stillbirths and attacking pregnant women.
- Asag: Linked to disease and illness.
- Namtaru: Associated with disease and misfortune.
- Gallu: Dragged people to the underworld.
- Alû: Caused nightmares and distress.
- Lilitu: Linked to night and harm.
- Sedu: Could be protective or harmful.
- Ida: Tied to death or illness.

All of them were called demons.

Originally, *"demon"* referred to destructive space rocks, but it evolved to mean *"evil"* or *"bad."*

The demon Lamashtu, depicted with a lioness's head and bird-like feet, was a story to explain infant mortality, not a real entity. When a mother's baby died in the womb it was said the demon Lamashtu took it.

A monster is scary; a demon is evil.

Chapter 11

Ark of the Covenant

In this chapter, I am focusing on what the Ark of the Covenant was and who commissioned it and why. The Bible describes two cherubim on its lid, yet their nature remains unclear. I will explore this in the next chapter. For now, we need to determine who ordered the Ark's creation and its purpose.

Based on my research, the Gods were the Anunnaki, meaning an Anunnaki God likely instructed its creation. Let us investigate whether the Anunnaki used or commissioned anything resembling a sacred box in ancient texts.

Sumerian and Akkadian mythology mention objects with parallels to the Ark.

The Tablets of Destiny, held by Gods like Enlil or Marduk, granted universal authority, symbolising divine power akin to the Ark's role in housing the Ten Commandments. Though not a box, their significance mirrors the Ark's sacred status. Similarly, the Me's, divine decrees governing civilisation, were bestowed by Enki and later transferred to Inanna.

The Ark of the Covenant

While not contained in a box, they represent divine knowledge given to humans, much like the Ark's role.

In Greek mythology, also tied to the Anunnaki, Pandora's Box, a divine container releasing evils, shares the concept of a sacred vessel, though its negative connotations differ from the Ark's divine presence.

Mesopotamian rituals involved transporting divine statues or sacred items in chests or palanquins, suggesting a portable sacred object like the Ark.

According to biblical chronology, the Ark was constructed around 1446–1400 BCE, after the Israelites' exodus from Egypt, during their time at Mount Sinai. As described in Exodus 25:10–22, God instructed Moses to build it shortly after the covenant and Ten Commandments were established. Some scholars suggest a later date, around the 13th century BCE, based on an alternative Exodus timeline, but the traditional dating places it 3,424–3,470 years ago, roughly 1,394–1,442 years before Jesus' birth.

Which Anunnaki Would Have Made the Ark?

Let us see who would have made the rules in the 10 Commandments; there are rules before the 10 Commandments called: Code of Hammurabi which were written by:
- Anu (sky God, father of the Gods)
- Enlil (God of wind and earth, Lord of the pantheon)
- Ea (Enki) (God of wisdom, water, and creation)
- Marduk (chief God of Babylon, patron of Hammurabi)
- Shamash (Utu) (sun God and God of justice; depicted handing laws to Hammurabi in the stele's relief)

The code was written approximately 3,780 years ago; interestingly Marduk's name is on there, he took over around 3000 BCE, which was around 5,000 years ago, so the time frame 3,780 years ago explains why his name was on the text along with Enlil who gave up his leader role to Marduk, thus Marduk would have been the one who wanted rules!

Otherwise we would have had rules before Marduk took over! The Code of Hammurabi has 282 rules, some are really complicated and even unfair; here is just one:

"Rule 209: If a man strikes a freeborn woman and causes her to miscarry, he pays 10 shekels of silver for her fetus. If the woman dies, his daughter is put to death."

Then approximately 304–465 years later we got the 10 Commandments.
- Code of Hammurabi: ~3,775–3,780 years ago
- Ten Commandments: ~3,471–3,315 years ago
- Ark of the Covenant: ~3,471–3,315 years ago

What is the point of putting the 10 Commandments in a chest when laws were already given out?
It suggests the Commandments were not just tablets.

But who would have built the Ark?
At this time, several Anunnaki figures were active. Enki, likely very old, may have died around then, maybe too old to focus on human conflicts. But before then Enlil might still have been alive, while Marduk, Enki's son, was rising to prominence as the *"most high."*

Inanna, Enlil's fierce granddaughter, had no qualms about killing humans.

Ninurta, Enlil's son, and Nergal, known as Hades and the destroyer, were also present.

Other Anunnaki and Igigi would have been restrained from commissioning such a device, and only two Gods ruled Israel: Enlil then later Marduk and, per the Hebrew Bible, the entity instructing the Ark's creation, identified as Yahweh.

As discussed in my chapter on Yahweh and the Vatican, Enlil and his family likely relocated to Greece, controlling Rome from there, leaving Marduk dominant in the Middle East.

Other Anunnaki Gods, though not in charge, maintained human armies opposing Marduk's forces. This points to Marduk as the likely commissioner of the Ark. But why a box? Why not use his advanced technology, like a flying craft, to aid his people directly?

The answer lies in King Anu's decree that humans should inherit the Earth. This did not stop Inanna from collaborating with kings like Sargon to win battles, but Marduk, with his son Nabu to help him, risked attack from rivals like Inanna if he intervened to help his humans with advanced technology. Providing humans with a device like the Ark allowed him to empower them indirectly.

To understand the Ark's purpose, let us examine its mentions across traditions.

In Islamic tradition, the Ark, called the *"Tabut"* in the Qur'an's Surah Al-Baqarah (2:248), symbolised divine favour during the time of the prophet Samuel and King Saul (Talut).

Its return confirmed Talut's leadership, carrying relics from Moses and Aaron, possibly the Ten Commandments, brought by angels to reassure the Israelites.

Like the Judeo-Christian narrative, it was a sacred chest symbolising God's covenant, guidance, and protection, constructed under divine command during Moses' era.

The Bible presents the Ark as a container for sacred relics, primarily the Ten Commandments, built at God's command to symbolise the covenant with the Israelites. Though not initially a weapon, it became associated with divine power, carried into battles to ensure victory through God's favour.

This raises questions: Why build a wooden box overlaid with gold, carried by priests, when the wheel existed?

Why not use a cart for easier transport, especially over rough terrain? They didn't have roads like we do.

The requirement for priests to carry the Ark, wearing specialised garments, suggests a deeper purpose. The High Priest's ephod, a sleeveless garment of fine linen with gold, blue, purple, and scarlet threads, featured onyx stones engraved with the names of Israel's tribes. Over it, a breastplate with twelve gemstones representing the tribes in four rows (sardius, topaz, carbuncle; emerald, sapphire, diamond; jacinth, agate, amethyst; beryl, onyx, jasper) was woven with gold.

A blue robe with gold bells and pomegranates, a linen tunic, a turban with a gold plate inscribed *"Holiness to the Lord,"* and a woven sash completed the attire.

Could these garments, incorporating gold, protect against radiation from the Ark?

Gold, due to its high density and atomic number, effectively shields against gamma rays and X-rays by absorbing and scattering high-energy photons.

It also blocks alpha and beta particles, though these require less dense materials.

However, gold is less effective against neutron radiation, which needs light atoms like boron or hydrogen. The gold in the priests' garments and the Ark's overlay might have offered some protection when closed, but opening it could expose people to harmful radiation, especially if it contained a radioactive source.

The Ark's design, carried on poles for smooth movement rather than on wheels, suggests it housed sensitive technology. Modern fragile items like electronics, explosives, or chemical solutions align with this idea. The Ark's lid, the mercy seat, was not mechanically locked but was restricted to authorised priests, implying delicate contents.

Non-canonical traditions mention items put in the Ark, like the Ten Commandments tablets, Aaron's rod, a pot of manna, a Torah scroll, shattered tablet pieces, anointing oil, or incense. These seem symbolic, unlikely to justify carrying a heavy gold-covered box, unless they were misunderstood technological components, perhaps batteries, chargers, or devices unfamiliar to ancient humans.

The Ark's power is evident in the biblical account of its capture by the Philistines (1 Samuel 4).

After defeating the Israelites at Ebenezer, the Philistines took the Ark, viewing it as a significant victory. However, they faced calamities: plagues, tumours, and rodents afflicted their cities, and their God Dagon's statue fell and broke in the Ark's presence. Believing it brought divine judgment, they returned it on a cow-pulled cart with gold offerings.

These events suggest radiation, particularly gamma or X-rays, emanating when the Ark was opened.

If the Ark functioned as a weapon, it might resemble modern technologies:

- **Directed Energy Weapon:** Emitting controlled bursts of gamma or X-rays to harm targets.
- **Portable Radiation Source:** Containing a radioactive material, weaponised to cause sickness.
- **Nuclear-like Device:** Emitting ionising radiation without exploding, causing localised effects.
- **Tesla-like Device:** Generating electromagnetic pulses or resonant frequencies to disrupt structures or biology.
- **Plasma-based Weapon:** Producing intense energy bursts, mimicking radiation exposure.
- **Unknown Ancient Technology:** A lost Anunnaki device generating focused energy.

The cherubim, with wings spread over the mercy seat, I cover them in the next chapter but are important for the Ark to be a weapon.

The priests' breastplate, with its gemstones, may have enabled communication with Marduk; crystals can be used as receivers and transmitters even without a battery!

This suggests the Ark was a sophisticated device, not merely a relic holder.

During the Ark's era, Middle Eastern Gods included:
- **Yahweh (Marduk):** Israel's God, tied to the Ark.
- **Baal (Unknown Anunnaki, possibly Nergal or Ninurta):** Canaanite storm and fertility God.
- **Asherah (Enlil's wife):** Canaanite mother Goddess, sometimes linked to Yahweh.
- **Marduk:** Babylon's chief God, controlling his original lands.
- **Ishtar (Inanna):** Babylonian Goddess of love and war, Marduk's enemy.
- **Dagon (Unknown Anunnaki):** Philistine agricultural God.
- **El (Enlil):** Canaanite chief God.
- **Chemosh, Hadad, Amun (Marduk in Egypt):** Other regional deities, some tied to Anunnaki.

In the ancient Near East, conflicts between cultures were seen as contests between their Gods' followers. Marduk likely commissioned the Ark to empower his Israelite followers against rival Anunnaki-led armies, such as Inanna's, without direct intervention, adhering to Anu's decree while countering threats.

In summary, I believe Marduk instructed his people to build the Ark as a technological device to secure victories against other Anunnaki Gods' human armies, combining sacred symbolism with advanced, possibly radioactive, functionality.

I will leave you with this; what happens if you mishandle the Ark:

Uzzah's Death: In 2 Samuel 6:6–7 (c. 1000 BCE), Uzzah, a priest or Levite, touched the Ark of the Covenant to steady it during transport on a cart, violating God's command that only Levites carry it by poles (Exodus 25:12–14, Numbers 4:5–6). God struck him dead for the unauthorised contact, showing the Ark's holiness and the need for strict obedience.

General Role of Priests/Levites: The Ark was carried by Levites (specifically Kohathites) using poles, as prescribed in Numbers 4:4–15 and Deuteronomy 10:8. They were responsible for transporting it during Israel's wanderings and into battle (e.g., Joshua 3:3–17, crossing the Jordan). Unauthorised handling or viewing could result in divine punishment (e.g., 1 Samuel 6:19, 70 men of Beth-Shemesh killed for looking into the Ark).

Later Fate: After Solomon placed the Ark in the Temple (c. 957 BCE, 1 Kings 8:6–11), priests no longer carried it regularly. The Ark's fate after the Babylonian destruction of Jerusalem (587 BCE) is unknown; no biblical record describes priests carrying it post-exile.

Chapter 12

Cherubim

What were the cherubim? Why do not we see them today, despite their prominence in the past when the Anunnaki were here? This offers our first clue about their nature.

Another question is, why should we care?

On the surface, cherubim seem less significant than figures like the Watchers or fallen angels, but I hope to show their importance in this chapter.

Mainstream interpretations, rooted in biblical texts, describe cherubim as angelic beings tasked with guarding sacred spaces and symbolising God's presence.
On the Ark of the Covenant, two golden cherubim adorned the lid, known as the mercy seat, their wings spread and facing each other, covering the sacred space.

They represented God's throne, with the Ark as His footstool and the space between them as his earthly dwelling.

Two cherubim on top of the Ark

In other biblical contexts, cherubim are guardians, such as those stationed at the Garden of Eden's entrance after Adam and Eve's expulsion, wielding a flaming sword to protect the Tree of Life (Genesis 3:24).

In Ezekiel, cherubim are complex, with multiple faces (man, lion, ox, eagle) and roles in divine movement.

Ancient art often depicts cherubim as winged creatures with human and animal features, symbolising God's sovereignty and holiness.

However, as I have shown in my other chapters, the idea of divine beings does not hold up. The Anunnaki were not divine but advanced beings. Unlike angels, who served as Anunnaki messengers, cherubim did not deliver messages or travel.

They were often depicted with wings, a trait shared with Anunnaki *"sky Gods"* and archangels, indicating flying craft. For example, 1 Enoch 39:3–4 describes Enoch being whisked into the heavens by a whirlwind, likely a spaceship:
"And in those days a whirlwind carried me off from the earth and set me down at the end of the heavens."

Similarly, 1 Enoch 14:8–9 recounts clouds, mist, stars, and winds lifting Enoch to heaven, and 2 Kings 2:11 describes Elijah ascending in a chariot of fire. These suggest advanced technology, not divine beings.
So, what were the cherubim? I propose they were not living beings but technological devices, possibly sentry weapons, based on their roles and descriptions. Let us explore this idea.

Protective guns sit on the top of the Ark

In biblical texts, cherubim consistently appear as guardians. At the Garden of Eden, they prevent re-entry with a flaming sword, suggesting an active defence mechanism.

On the Ark of the Covenant, their wings cover the mercy seat, protecting sacred relics like the Ten Commandments and possibly serving as part of a defensive system. The Ark, carried into battles for divine favour, was linked to supernatural power, hinting that the cherubim were more than decorative.

They were not alive on the Ark because it would have been mentioned and the thought of having two living beings just sitting on the top of a chest is not logical.

The flaming sword in Genesis could symbolise an energy weapon, like a laser or plasma beam, reacting to threats, akin to modern sentry guns that detect and respond to unauthorised access.

The cherubim's wings might have functioned as antennas, conductors, or energy focusers, directing radiation, electromagnetic fields, or sound waves to deter enemies.

Their symmetrical placement could channel energy, like electrodes in modern devices, or act as capacitors storing electrical charge. Alternatively, the wings might have dissipated heat, like heat-sinks if the Ark generated intense energy.

The cherubim's design suggests they were integral to the Ark's potential as a weapon or defence system.

The cherubim's static nature supports this view. Mentioned about 90 times in the Bible, they never walk or speak with humans like angels such as Gabriel or Michael.

They remain stationary, like sentry devices guarding sacred spaces. However, some texts describe dynamic roles: In Ezekiel, cherubim are part of a divine chariot with wheels within wheels, moving without turning, suggesting advanced technology, possibly a craft with defensive capabilities.

In Psalms 18:10, God rides upon a cherub, implying a connection to celestial movement, perhaps a spacecraft equipped with weapons.

I propose the cherubim were Anunnaki-designed weapons, like laser-equipped sentry guns on their craft, guarding critical locations day and night.

The Anunnaki, capable of space travel, had the technology to create such devices. The flaming sword aligns with this, representing a high-energy defence system.

To summarise, the cherubim were not living beings but technological devices, likely weapons, guarding sacred spaces like the Ark or the Garden of Eden. Their winged depictions and static roles suggest they were advanced Anunnaki creations, ensuring protection without the need for constant divine presence.

Chapter 13

Heaven

Why do we look up to heaven, whether we are in Australia or elsewhere? The simple answer is that ancient texts describe the Gods ascending to heaven.

Before diving in, let us explore why the word *"heaven"* is so prevalent. It is rooted in the Bible, though older texts mention it too.

If we pray to heaven, why do not we pray to the great lord Enki, despite his prominence in those ancient texts just like the word heaven, yet we use *"heaven"* because of its biblical weight.

The Oxford Dictionary defines heaven as:
A place regarded in various religions as the abode of God (or Gods), angels, and the good after death, often depicted above the sky.
The sky, perceived as a vault containing the sun, moon, stars, and planets.

This definition points to heaven as space; heaven has celestial bodies such as the sun, stars and moon.

So why do we imagine it as a realm for the dead? I will address that later. First, let us examine biblical and older texts to uncover the truth.

In Revelation 21 (Young's Literal Translation), John describes:

"And I saw a new heaven and a new earth, for the first heaven and the first earth did pass away, and the sea is not any more; and I, John, saw the holy city new Jerusalem coming down from God out of the heaven... and I heard a great voice out of the heaven, saying, 'Lo, the tabernacle of God is with men, and He will tabernacle with them...'"

Breaking this down, John sees a new heaven and earth, with the old ones and the sea passing away. From a spaceship in space (heaven), Earth's rotation would make land and sea appear and disappear. The *"new Jerusalem"* descending from heaven suggests John was with an Anunnaki God in space, returning to Earth.

The *"great voice out of the heaven"* speaking of the tabernacle, a device connecting God to his people, implies a communication system, like a radio, used from space. In Judaism, the Tabernacle (Mishkan) was a portable sanctuary housing the Ark of the Covenant and possibly a radio within it; the Tabernacle was built per divine instructions (Exodus 25–31, 35–40).

In Christianity, it foreshadows Jesus' presence (John 1:14) or refers to the Eucharistic tabernacle. Broadly, it symbolises God's chance to be with humans without him being there in person, but I propose it was a technological device for divine communication.

Young's Literal Translation also warns in Deuteronomy 4:19: *"And lest thou lift up thine eyes towards the heavens, and hast seen the sun, and the moon, and the stars, all the host of the heavens, and thou hast been forced, and hast bowed thyself to them... which Jehovah thy God hath apportioned to all the peoples under the whole heavens."*

As I have shown, Jehovah was Enki (in another chapter), and we can see the Bible drew from the older tablets and stories, for example. In the Enuma Elish tablets:
"Then were created the Gods in the midst of [heaven], Lakhmu and Lakhamu were called into being..."

These *"Gods"* are planets *Lakhmu and Lakhamu* are Mars and Venus, showing the Anunnaki personified celestial bodies.

Another text, from A New Boundary Stone of Nebuchadrezzar I (W. J. Hinke, 1907), describes Enlil as:
"the exalted lord, ruler of heaven and earth, Prince, lord of all King of the great Gods, who in heaven and earth."

This predates the Bible, yet calls Enlil, an Anunnaki, ruler of heaven and earth. This points out he operated from a spacecraft in orbit, as heaven (space) would not be a domain to control otherwise.

Here is ancient text where Enoch goes into heaven and sees what we would say is a spacecraft.

From Apocryphal Ancient Text: Book of Enoch (1 Enoch 14)
In this ancient Jewish text (c. 3rd–1st century BCE), *Enoch is called by clouds and mist, hastened by stars, lightnings, and winds that lift him upward into heaven.*

He sees a crystal wall with tongues of fire, enters a house of crystal with a tessellated crystal floor and ceiling like paths of stars/lightnings, with fiery cherubim and blazing portals.

The house is hot as fire and cold as ice.

He then enters a greater house of flames, with a fiery floor, lightning/stars above, and a crystal throne with wheels shining like the sun, from which streams of fire issue. The throne holds the Great Glory, too magnificent for angels or flesh to behold, with flaming fire around.

Elements like the lifting winds/lightnings (propulsion), crystal materials (advanced tech), and fiery throne (command centre/reactor) could suggest a spaceship or high-tech vehicle.

Who else was mentioned in heaven?
Cuneiform Parallels to the Old Testament (Robert William Rogers) notes:
"Ishtar, the queen of heaven, may she protect my brother."

Ishtar (Inanna), called queen of heaven post-flood, further ties Anunnaki to space. Some Sumerian translators confuse *"heaven"* with Earth's sky, as in Enlil and Sud (c.1.2.2):
"The dust from their march reached high into the sky like rain clouds."

Yet Enki and the World Order (c.1.1.3) uses *"heavens"* for sky:
"He called to the rain of the heavens."

Is it possible the person that translated the last passage got it wrong? *"He called to the rain of the heavens."*

The original Sumerian word used in the tablet for *"heavens"* in the phrase *"He called to the rain of the heavens"* is most likely an, as derived from the context of Enki and the World Order (ETCSL 1.1.3).

The term an appears frequently in Sumerian texts to denote *"heaven," "sky,"* or a divine upper realm. The answer is yes, the word An means heaven and or sky; it is like us saying the word *"shine"*, it could mean something is lit up and shine or it could not be lit but just reflective.

Since space does not rain, *"heavens"* here likely means Earth's sky, but other texts clarify heaven as space.
Enlil and Ninlil (c.1.2.1) states:
"Lord who makes flax grow, lord who makes barley grow, you are lord of heaven, lord plenty, lord of the earth! Enlil in heaven."

This confirms Enlil was in space, likely on a spacecraft, as orbiting is easier than hovering in Earth's atmosphere. The Sumerian term *"An"* denotes *"heaven,"* referring to celestial realms or divine spaces, often tied to Nibiru, the Anunnaki's home planet.

Translators sometimes avoid *"Nibiru,"* opting for *"heaven"* to align with spiritual interpretations, obscuring literal space travel.
For instance, in **Adapa and the Food of Life** (Tablet 2), Adapa (biblical Adam) is summoned to Nibiru by King Anu:
"Adapa, the son of Ea... has broken the wing of the South wind... When Anu heard these words... 'Let some one bring him,' Likewise Ea, who knows the heaven... The road to Heaven he made him take, and to Heaven he ascended."

Reworded for clarity:
"Adapa, the son of Ea, has broken the wing of the South wind... Ea, (Enki) who knows Nibiru... The road to Nibiru he made him take, and to space he ascended."

This suggests a physical journey to a celestial destination, not a spiritual ascent.

Similarly, **Inana and Enki (c.1.3.1)** describes Inanna boarding the *"Boat of Heaven,"* which leaves the quay, implying a spaceship departing for space:

"Holy Inana had gathered up the divine powers and embarked onto the Boat of Heaven. The Boat of Heaven had already left the quay."

The text later asks, *"Where has the Boat of Heaven reached now?"* with the response, *"It has just now reached the … Quay,"* possibly omitting a term like *"Nibiru"* due to the translators' caution 100–200 years ago, when suggesting extraterrestrial travel was controversial.

The Hittite Version of the Hurrian Kumarbi solidifies this: *"Alalu was king in heaven. Alalu is sitting on the throne, and the mighty Anu… bows down to his feet… In the ninth year, Anu fought against Alalu… he overcame Alalu, so that he fled from him and went down to the dark earth."*

Here, *"heaven"* is Nibiru or space, not an invisible realm. Several figures in ancient texts ascended to heaven without dying, likely via Anunnaki craft:
- **Enoch (1 Enoch):** Taken to heaven and returned.
- **Elijah (2 Kings 2:11):** Ascended in a fiery chariot, expected to return.
- **Adapa** (Mesopotamian): Visited Anu on Nibiru and returned.
- **Etana** (Mesopotamian): Flew to heaven on an eagle.
- Arjuna and Yudhishthira (Hindu): Journeyed to heaven and returned.
- **Muhammad** (Islamic): Ascended and returned in the Isra and Mi'raj.

No one has gone to heaven since the Anunnaki ceased taking humans. Modern claims of seeing God rely on feelings, not evidence.

The Sumerian tablets, numbering around 2 million (equivalent to 606,061 Bible-sized pages), far outweigh the Bible's 1,400 pages, providing richer context from Sumerian, Akkadian, Babylonian, Assyrian, Egyptian, Hittite, Greek, Latin, and Arabic sources.

The idea of heaven as a place for the dead is a later construct. My Hell chapter and three-hour documentary Everything You Need to Know About Spirits explain that the dead persist at different frequencies, not in heaven or hell, as confirmed by clairvoyants, mediums, and spiritualists.

During the Scientific Revolution (17th century), *"space"* began to describe the expanse beyond Earth's atmosphere, a concept emerging when tablets were first translated around 1824, though not fully used throughout the world.

The Anunnaki named heaven as space, describing it as the domain of the sun, moon, stars, and their travels. They lived there, traversed it, and ruled it. Heaven is space, not a magical realm for the dead.

King James Bible
"And lest thou lift up thine eyes unto heaven, and when thou seest the sun, and the moon, and the stars"

If we believe this, it means we can see heaven, because we can see the sun and the moon and the stars; of course it is not heaven, it is space.

But what about the word heavens?

There are many references to heavens, yet there is only one space!

The Anunnaki Gods crossed the heavens to get to Earth; I suggest one heaven is above the asteroid belt and the other is below; however there is a possibility that they may have assigned *"space"* around planets, like we have airspace, which we have worked out which part of our skies belong to which country.

The same could have been done by the Anunnaki Gods.

Chapter 14

Hell - Underworld

In this chapter, I will explore the origins of Hell, its earliest mentions and the cultures that shaped the concept. My goal is to reveal where the idea of Hell came from and what it truly was, using evidence no other researcher has presented in this way. Forgive the brief moment of self-praise.

The concept of Hell as a place of punishment for the wicked after death has deep roots across various cultures. Let us start with its earliest mentions:

Sumerian (c. 3500–3000 BCE): The Sumerians described a netherworld called Kur or Irkalla, originally ruled only by the Anunnaki Goddess Ereshkigal, sister of Inanna. All souls went there, regardless of their deeds, to exist in a shadowy state.

Ancient Egypt (c. 3100 BCE): The Duat, detailed in the Book of the Dead, was the realm of the dead. Souls faced challenges and judgment, though not necessarily punishment.

Ancient Greece (c. 8th century BCE): Hades, ruled by the God of the same name, housed all souls. Tartarus, a deeper region, was reserved for punishing the wicked, as seen in Homer's epics.

Ancient Judaism (c. 1200–1000 BCE): Sheol, in the Hebrew Bible, was a silent abyss where all the dead went. Over time, it evolved into a place of differing fates for the righteous and the wicked.

Christianity (c. 1st century CE): The New Testament introduces Gehenna (e.g., Matthew 5:22, 10:28)—a fiery place of punishment. It was based on the Valley of Hinnom, historically linked to child sacrifice.

Islam (c. 610 CE): Jahannam, described in the Qur'an (e.g., Surah 4:56, 15:43–44), is a place of severe torment for sinners and non-believers.

Hinduism and Buddhism (c. 1500–500 BCE): Naraka, found in texts like the Puranas, is a realm of torment within the cycle of samsara.

Zoroastrianism (c. 1000–600 BCE): The Avesta describes a realm of torment awaiting the wicked after death.

Like me, you may believe that the earliest sources are the most accurate. Since many claim that God sends the wicked to Hell, let us examine the earliest mentions of Gods, as these early concepts are often closer to the original:

- Sumerians (c. 3500–3000 BCE)
- Ancient Egypt (c. 3100 BCE)
- Indus Valley Civilisation (c. 2500–1900 BCE)
- Akkadians (c. 2334–2154 BCE)
- Ancient China – Shang Dynasty (c. 1600–1046 BCE)
- Ancient Greece – Mycenaean (c. 1600–1100 BCE)
- Hittites (c. 1600–1178 BCE)
- Hebrews (c. 1200–1000 BCE)

- Vedic Civilisation (c. 1500–500 BCE)
- Ancient Persia – Zoroastrianism (c. 1000–600 BCE)
- Olmecs (c. 1400–400 BCE)
- Ancient Rome (c. 753–509 BCE)
- Christianity (c. 1st century CE)
- Catholicism (c. 4th century CE)
- Islam (c. 610 CE)
- Latter-day Saints (c. 1820s CE)

Later deities like Yahweh (Exodus 20:3), Ahura Mazda, Allah (Surah Al-Ikhlas 112:1–4), and the Christian God (Matthew 4:10) demanded exclusive worship and rejected all other Gods. In contrast, earlier cultures such as the Sumerians, Egyptians, Akkadians, Chinese, Greeks, and Hittites acknowledged multiple Gods even with one being the most high, Enlil.

Would an almighty creator really allow early humans to worship *"false"* Gods from the very beginning only to later condemn them to Hell for it?

The earliest temples were built for the Anunnaki, Enki, Enlil, Nanna, and Ninurta, not a singular deity. Why would a supreme being permit this from the start, only to later declare these Gods false and warn of Hell?

The New Testament and Qur'an (e.g., Surah Al-Bayyinah 98:6) both speak of eternal punishment for non-believers. Yet no God appeared with miracles or clear proof of supremacy, unlike Enlil, who was described in ancient texts as *"the highest"* seated on a throne of lapis lazuli.

Hell's Location in the oldest Ancient Texts

In **Enlil in the E-kur** (c.4.05.1), we find:
"Enlil, holy Uraš is favoured with beauty for you; you are greatly suited for the Abzu, the holy throne... you refresh yourself in the deep underworld, the holy chamber."

This connects the underworld to the Abzu (Africa), a subterranean realm.

In **Dumuzid and Ĝeštin-ana** (c.1.4.1.1):
"The demons entered Unug and seized holy Inana... 'Come on, Inana... descend to the underworld... Go to the dwelling of Ereshkigal—descend to the underworld.'"

Inanna's Descent to the Netherworld adds:
"To the netherworld, the land without return, Inanna set her mind... Ereshkigal is queen of the underworld, she who holds the laws of the land."

Ereshkigal ruled the underworld and is identified with the Abzu (Africa) and oversaw the dead. My documentary Everything You Need to Know About Spirits explains how the Anunnaki understood spirits.

After the flood (c. 10,000 BCE), Ningishzida (Thoth) recorded out-of-body experiences involving orbs in the Emerald Tablets of Thoth. This led to mummification and the Book of the Dead, showing the Anunnaki's growing interest with the afterlife.

Before the flood, during their 445,000-year presence, the Anunnaki buried their dead simply with stones and two ply cloth. Afterward, they began to understand orbs, possibly living plasma entities connected to the pineal gland that reincarnate and carry memory.

Was Ereshkigal judging humans or divine beings?

She managed primarily human souls but also held authority over deceased Gods and demigods.

In **The Death of Ur-Namma** :
"After the offerings were presented... the Anuna seated Ur-Namma on a great dais of the netherworld... At the command of Ereshkigal, with (?) Gilgamesh, his beloved brother, he will pass the judgments of the netherworld."

So why focus on human souls, whose lifespans were short, 40 years, or 8 months by Anunnaki life span?
The orbs were more significant. They survived death and reincarnated. Ereshkigal likely catered to these entities.

In Norse mythology, Valkyries carried the dead to Valhalla, but I argue they actually transported the bodies to Ereshkigal in the Abzu. Why bother with bodies if the spirits (orbs) had already left?

In the Abzu, statues were made for the righteous to *"live forever,"* while those of the wicked were destroyed. This tradition likely applied to demigods, like Gilgamesh, whose deaths carried more meaning due to their leadership roles.

The Death of Gilgamesh states:
"Enlil... has made kingship your destiny, but not eternal life... The darkest day of humans awaits you now... When a funerary statue is made... mighty youths... will form a semicircle at the door-jambs..."

As a demigod, Gilgamesh received a statue to preserve his legacy, unlike ordinary humans.

So why did Ereshkigal's underworld resemble a prison?

In Inanna's Descent, Inanna dies and is only revived by Enki, but she must provide a substitute; her beloved Dumuzi was selected for six months, then Ĝeštin-ana who was Inanna's human helper stayed there the other six months in Hell.

Similarly, Nergal, Ereshkigal's consort, visits for seven days and must return, bound by divine law.

The underworld, ruled by Ereshkigal (Female) and Nergal (male), became associated with fire, torment, and confinement, which matches the translations and these ideas that carried over into later traditions.

Cultures with underworld deities, **female** rulers of the underworld:
- Sumerian: Ereshkigal
- Greek: Persephone
- Norse: Hel
- Aztec: Mictecacihuatl
- Etruscan: Vanth
- Polynesian: Hine-nui-te-pō

Male rulers:
- Sumerian: Nergal
- Greek: Hades
- Egyptian: Osiris
- Hindu: Yama
- Maya: Ah Puch
- Aztec: Mictlantecuhtli
- Roman: Pluto
- Celtic: Arawn
- Japanese: Enma

Cultures with **both**: Sumerian, Greek, Aztec, Norse, Etruscan.

Notably, Nergal and Hades are both linked to three-headed dogs. Nergal's appears in carvings at Nimrud's Northwest Palace.
Cerberus, Hades' guard dog, appears in Hesiod's Theogony, Apollodorus' Library, Virgil's Aeneid, and Greek art.
The Sumerian word for souls *"gidim"* (shades) closely resembles *"Hades"* minus the *"s."*

Here is a real carving of Nergal with the three-headed dog from ancient times; you will see a lot of symbols on the carving, each means something which I have covered in videos.

You will see Ereshkigal with her pets in the background, whereas her sister Inanna is carved normally with one foot on either a lion or a person.

Actual carving of Nergal (God of the underworld) and his 3 headed dog.

Comparing the Ancient and Modern Underworlds

Sumerian Kur:
- Dark, lifeless, and gloomy
- Gated and judged by Ereshkigal and Nergal
- Souls known as shades
- Separate from the living
- Required rituals

Modern Hell:
- Fiery, torment-filled
- Eternal punishment
- Separation from God
- Populated by demons
- Inescapable
- Structured into levels (e.g., Dante's Inferno)
- Judged by a supreme deity

Modern concepts of Hell exaggerate Kur's features, layering on fire, eternal punishment, and divine wrath. But Hell as the underworld originated in the Abzu, managed by Ereshkigal and Nergal. Over time, evolving stories across cultures shaped the Hell we think of today.

When you die, you do not go to Hell or Heaven. You remain here. Spirits exist at different frequencies.

The God and Goddess judged your life; if it was good a statue of you was put out, but if you were bad they would smash it, stopping your immortality.

Chapter 15

Spirits

Was there really a big bang and what is that got to do with spirits?
It might be when spirits first started.
Stephen Hawking suggested that if the universe is expanding then if we rewind it we would see it go back to a single point of time.
Is that the only reference we have to the Big Bang? Actually, the Emerald Tablets of Thoth talk about the Big Bang. Thoth was a God in ancient Egyptian times.

The text for the Emerald Tablets of Thoth (Thoth was Nigishzed, son of Enki, brother of Marduk) first appeared in a number of early medieval Arabic sources, the oldest of which dates to the late 8th or 9th century.

It was translated into Latin several times in the 12th and 13th century. Numerous interpretations and commentaries followed.
There were 10 tablets which were divided into 13 parts. The last two are so great and far-reaching in their importance that at present it is forbidden to release into the world at large, so it is claimed. Because of these translations by different people over centuries we can say with some degree of certainty that the translations copied something.

Sadly the original tablets have been lost or hidden away from view.

This is the text about the start of the universe from the Emerald Tablets.

"In the beginning there was void and nothingness, a timeless, spaceless, nothingness and into the nothingness came a thought, purposeful or pervading and it filled the void. There existed no matter, only force, a movement, a vortex of vibration, of purposeful thought that filled the void."

That's pretty impressive text for over 1,200 years ago when they didn't even know what space was!

Although the creation of the universe in the tablets come from a thought, it is the only thing we have to go on and it actually makes sense because everything in the physical world has a top, bottom and two sides, yet the universe may not.

Only a thought is endless. The tablets go on to say:

"In the beginning there was eternal thought, and for thought to be eternal time must exist, so into the all-pervading thought grew the law of time. I, time which exists through all space, floating in a smooth rhythmic motion that is eternally in a state of fixation.

Time changes not, but all things change in time, for time is the force that holds events separate, each in its proper place.
Time is not in motion, but ye move through time as your consciousness moves from one event to another. I, by time ye exist, all in all an eternal one existence."

How can you argue that the tablets are wrong when way back then they did not even know what a universe was, let alone how it could have started?

There are two types of Emerald Tablets, you have the older latin on which I'll put here the translations of:

The Emerald Tablet

(A classic English translation based on the Latin version)

1. True it is, without falsehood, certain and most true.
2. That which is above is like to that which is below, and that which is below is like to that which is above, to accomplish the miracles of the One Thing.
3. And as all things were from the One, by the meditation of the One, so all things have their birth from this One Thing by adaptation.
4. The Sun is its father, the Moon its mother.
5. The Wind carried it in its womb, the Earth is its nurse.
6. The Father of all perfection in the whole world is here.
7. Its force or power is entire if it be converted into Earth.
8. Separate the Earth from the Fire, the subtle from the gross, sweetly and with great ingenuity.
9. It ascends from the Earth to the Heaven, and again it descends to the Earth, and receives the force of things superior and inferior.
10. By this means, you shall have the glory of the whole world, and thereby all obscurity shall fly from you.
11. Its force is above all force, for it vanquishes every subtle thing and penetrates every solid thing.
12. So was the world created.
13. From this are and do come admirable adaptations, of which the process is here in this.

14. Hence am I called Thrice-Greatest Hermes, having the three parts of the philosophy of the whole world.
15. That which I have to say is completed concerning the Operation of the Sun.

The other translations are from **Maurice Doreal** (real name Claude Doggins) in the early 20th century.
These are called Emerald tablets of Thoth. (Earlier I showed you some of the translation)

1925: Doreal claims to have entered the Great Pyramid of Giza, where he discovered the physical Emerald Tablets. He then claims to have translated them and taken the tablets back to their hiding place.
There is no archaeological or scholarly evidence to support this claim.

However, as you read earlier Doreal talks about the start of the universe from a thought.

We didn't know the universe possibly started from a single point until Edwin Hubble (1929) provided the first observational evidence that the universe is indeed expanding by measuring the redshift of galaxies. This was a massive scientific breakthrough that moved the idea from theory to observed fact.

So, either Doreal was just making up a lucky guess 4 years before mainstream even thought of it, or he did have some insight.

1925: No records of Doreal visiting Egypt or mentioning pyramids/tablets. His later narratives describe it as a solo "astral" or physical entry.

I've read the translations of the Emerald tablets of Thoth, was Doreal making it up?
I'm a fan of evidence and I don't believe things easily without evidence.
I have read the Emerald Tablets of Thoth many, many times and have found information within it that only a genius would have added to it, or it was true.
For example Doreal talks about formless entities that came from the void, remember the Anunnaki called the emptyness of space, a void!
Here's what Doreal says on how were spirits created.

The tablets say this; this is a spirit talking to Thoth:

"Far beyond time we come, O man, travelled we from beyond the space-time. I, from the place of infinity's end, when ye and all of thy brethren were formless, formed forth were we from the order of all, not as men are we, though once we too were as men. Out of the great void were we formed, forth in order and by law, for know ye that that which is formed truly is formless, having form only to thine eyes."

I would say they were energy when the universe began and then over time had bodies and then over a longer period of time they shed those bodies and became energy again.
Energy is like an orb, the type that people have filmed.

There is way more in the Emerald tablets, such as another entity that would would call the Djinn, in the Emerald tablets I worked out the light beings and Djinn had been fighting each other since the dawn of time.

From my own perspective, Doreal was way ahead of his time in understanding ancient Egypt, Spirits, Reincarnation among many other subjects that are covered in his 'translations'. Anyone that knows me or has listened to me do live chats, knows I am the first person to debunk people, I've pretty much debunked most people, see my many hours long debunking videos. But the Emerald tablets of Thoth are too advanced for someone back in the late 1920s, far too advanced, even me, who's been researching is still learning from them.

Moving on to the orbs.

Pastor Monzel Ford says as he was sleeping one night last week his home surveillance camera motion detector kept going off. So from bed he pulled out his phone and looked at the living room:
"This orb, this imagery just hovering in my living room. No one else was there, it was not a flash light or passing headlights and Pastor Ford thinks it was too big to be a dust particle. He walked into the living room watching the live feed on his phone.

But when I went out there I could not physically see what I am looking at in the live feed. So now I am like whoa. The orb came and went for hours at one point splitting into several shapes.
That is when I am like nope, nope, nope, nope, nope, something is going out here, something is going here. But it was not until we got settled and my kids were playing in their room one day and they ran out of there screaming because they saw something and that is when we went and got security cameras."

The TV show **Skinwalker Ranch** has captured orbs.

"We have got all those new cameras out at the homesteads, so I get plenty of critter activity. You know what it looks like when you have got an old moth or some kind of insect or a piece of debris flying across your field of view. But I have got something here that does not fit in. Really? Yeah, happened just last night, after our experiment. What on earth is that? The hell is that? Okay, so let us play this through and I really want your thoughts on what this might be. No, it is behind the tree, so it is far enough away."

Many people with night vision camera's have caught them moving around, there's even camera's on the outside of a chruch that captured an orb flying right through the church wall and was picked up by the security camera inside!

There are two types of light energy orbs. There are darker ones. I will cover that a bit later. The first light energy beings that I hear are the size of basketballs.

I believe there are nine in total. These control the smaller orbs that you may have seen in videos.

The smaller orbs are about the size of a tennis ball. The nine large orbs that are the basketball size are in control of everything. They consist of seven that guide the smaller orbs. The remaining two are the leaders of everything, and dare I say, the underworld.

The seven that teach the smaller ones are numbered. This is what the tablet says.

Thoth is talking. *'For the Lords of Amenti, learned I the wisdom I gave unto men. The masters are they of the great secret wisdom. Brought from the future of infinity's end, seven are they, the Lords of Amenti, overlords they of the children of the morning, sun, and the cycles. Masters of wisdom formed are they as the children of men? Three, four, five, six, seven, eight, and nine are the titles of the masters of men.*

Far from the future, formless yet forming, come they as the teachers for the children of men. Live they forever, yet not of the living, bound to life and yet free from death. Rule they forever with infinite wisdom, bound yet not to bound to the dark halls of death. Life they have in them, yet life that is not life. Free from all of the Lords of all.

Far from them came the fourth of the Lords, instruments they have, instruments they of the power of yore. Vast in their countenance, yet hidden in smalls, formed by the forming, known yet unknown.' Orb number three holds the key of all the hidden magic. *'Creator of the halls of the dead, sending forth power, shrouding with darkness, binding the souls of the children of men.*
Sending the darkness, binding the soul force, director of negative to the children of men. The job of the fourth orb, he who loses the power, Lord he of life to the children of men. Light in his body, flame in his countenance, freer of souls to the children of men.'

Number five's job is the master, the Lord of magic, key to the word that resounds among men.
The sixth orb's job is the Lord of light, the hidden pathway, part of the souls of the children of men.

Seven is he who Lord of the vastness, master of space and the key of times. Eight is he who orders the progress, weighs and balances the journeys of man. Nine is the father, vast of the countenance, forming and changing from out of the formless.

I will explain more about the orbs numbered one and two later on, but for now we can see there is a council of seven light energy beings that explain to the smaller orbs what job they will have to do when they join with a human or another creature that is capable of having a light energy being merge with them.

Who does the spirit join with us? We can look elsewhere to find the answer.

The idea that the soul (rūḥ) enters the fetus at 120 days (approximately 4 months) comes from authentic hadiths (sayings of the Prophet Muhammad), not from a verse in the Qur'an itself.
Key Hadith (Sahih al-Bukhari and Sahih Muslim):
The Prophet said:
"Each of you is gathered as a creation in the womb of his mother for forty days as a drop of fluid, then he becomes a clot for a similar period, then a chewed-like lump for a similar period. Then Allah sends an angel who is commanded with four words: to write his deeds, his livelihood, his death, and whether he will be happy or miserable. Then the soul is breathed into him."
— Sahih al-Bukhari 3327, Sahih Muslim 2643

This timeline adds up:

- 40 days (nutfah) + 40 days ('alaqah) + 40 days (mudghah) = 120 days
- After this, the soul is breathed in.

"Then the soul is breathed into him." is when the orb joins the fetus.

When the age of a fetus reaches about 120 days, it no longer remains a pre-human living object; rather, it becomes a living human being. At this point, all organ differentiation is almost completed and the child acquires the shape of a human body.
More importantly, now that the soul has entered the body, the fetus is truly human. In the case of premature births that survive, the soul enters just prior to birth.

The question then is, how does a light energy being join with a fetus?
The entity connects with the pineal gland.

The pineal gland is a small, pea-shaped gland in the brain. Its function is not fully understood.
Researchers do know that it produces and regulates some hormones, including melatonin.

Melatonin is best known for the role it plays in regulating sleep patterns. Sleep patterns are also called circadian rhythms. However, cultural traditions attribute to the pineal gland an important role for spiritual experiences.

Mediumship and spirit possession are cultural phenomena found worldwide which have been described as having dissociative and psychotic-like characteristics, but with non-pathological aspects.

A sympathetic activation pattern in response to spirit possession has been reported in some studies. In ancient Egypt, the pineal gland was known as the *"seat of the spirit"* or the *"soul"*. They used the third eye as a route to higher awareness and consciousness.

The Buddhists related it to spiritual awakening. The Hindus connect it to the third eye which represents intuition and clairvoyance. Jesus said that the eye is the lamp of the body and if the eye is clear, your body will be filled with light. This relates to the eye of intuition, pineal gland, and seeing things clearly and in truth.

Sadly fluoride is likely to cause decreased melatonin production and to have other effects on normal pineal function, which in turn could contribute to a variety of effects in humans.

Have you ever wondered why we have fluoride in our tap water?
They have been putting it in our water for decades; this is *their* reason why they add fluoride.
Adding fluoride to the water supply reduces the incidence of tooth decay. Fluoride protects teeth from decay by demineralisation and remineralisation.

There is no way our governments want to help our teeth; since when do they care about our health?

They tax everything; why are they not taxing us for the fluoride? Because when you research where that fluoride comes from, you will know. I will not say it here but let us just say they want to get rid of it, so they put it in our water and that problem goes away and also it dumbs us down.

A study in 2019 by Cambridge University states, *"Fluoride levels in drinking water were associated with an increased risk of dementia in women."*

There are other studies that show too much fluoride can lead to dental fluorosis or skeletal fluorosis, which can damage bones and joints.

As you can see, fluoride is not really helping us at all. I have Horus, in ancient Egypt, symbol representing protection, health, and restoration.

According to Egyptian myth, Horus lost his left eye in a struggle with Seth. Eye of Horus, I was magically restored by a pha, and this restoration came to symbolise the process of making whole and healing. For this reason, the symbol was often used in amulets.

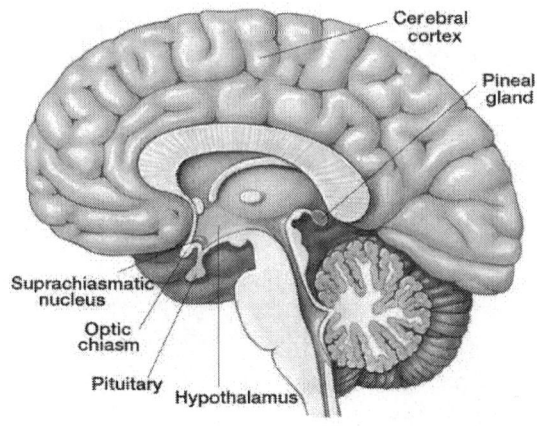

But if we look at a cross-section of the brain compared to the Eye of Horus, then it seems there is more to the Eye of Horus than just him losing an eye. The gland has amazing unique properties.

This is what the National Library of Medicine states.

"A new form of biomineralisation has been studied in the pineal gland of the human brain. It consists of small crystals

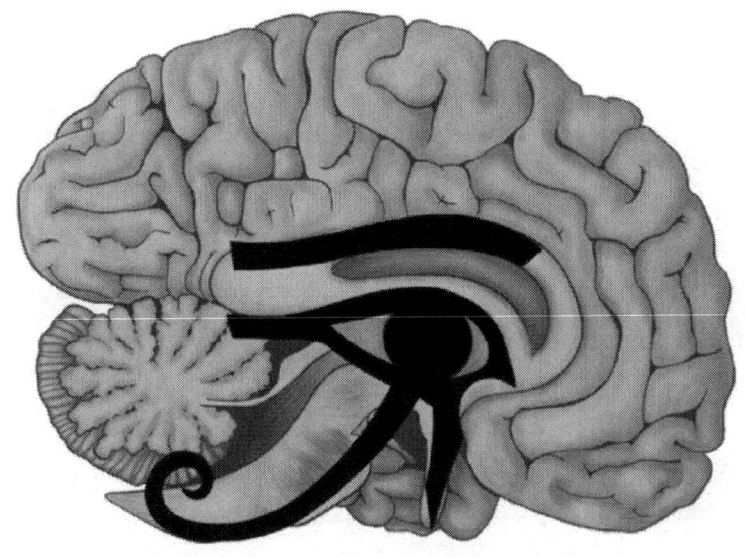

The Eye of Horus over the same location as the Pineal Gland.

that are less than 20 micron in length and that are completely distinct from the often observed Mulberry-type hydroxyapatite concretions.

A special procedure was developed for isolation of the crystals from the organic matter in the pineal gland. Cubic, hexagonal, and cylindrical morphologies have been identified using scanning electron microscopy.

The crystal edges were sharp whereas their surfaces were very rough. Energy-dispersive spectroscopy showed that the crystals contained only the elements calcium, carbon, and oxygen.
Selected area electron diffraction and near-infrared Raman spectroscopy established that the crystals were calcite.

With the exception of the otoconia structure of the inner ear. This is the only known non-pathological occurrence of calcite in the human body. The calcite microcrystals are probably responsible for the previously observed second harmonic generation in pineal tissue sections.

The complex texture structure of the microcrystals may lead to crystallographic symmetry breaking and possible piezoelectricity, as is the case with otoconia. It is believed that the presence of two different crystalline compounds in the pineal gland is biologically significant, suggesting two entirely different mechanisms of formation and biological functions.

Studies directed toward the elucidation of the formation and functions, and possible non-thermal interaction with external electromagnetic fields are currently in progress."

The part where they say non-thermal interaction with external electromagnetic fields are currently in progress is really important because the presence of calcite crystals in the pineal gland may turn it into a type of receiver that tunes into different frequencies in a manner similar to a radio receiver.

This may offer the beginnings of a scientific explanation that ties the pineal gland to receiving messages from spirit or allowing it to connect to it.

During the life connected with you, the entity knows everything you do.
It hears your thoughts, your feelings, it sees your actions but it never judges you. A light-being entity is there to learn, gain wisdom and extend to a higher plane; more on that later. But it does not know right from wrong. The spirit could be inside a murderer and will simply learn from that person.

But when it goes around again, reincarnation, the next time it might join with a murder victim; it does not care as long as it learns.

Imagine the spirit as a computer hard drive. Everything you do can be saved on it.

But if you take that hard drive with your files, we shall call them memories, onto another computer, the next computer can see the files, memories, that was in the older computer.

It does not mean the new computer created those files. It just means it can access the files. A light-being entity, spirit, is just like that when it joins with another person.

That person may see a memory of a past life, but it is not their life, it was belonged to someone else.

A lot of people get confused by this. They believe it was their own life that they lived. When the brain starts to die, the spirit entity leaves the body.

At this point the person that died is in control of the entity. The hard drive is full of the person that died. There appears to be another entity that has been around for a long time. It could have also been created at the same time as the light energy beings. This other type of entity has been called "Djinn". Some people say they are demons.

I believe I am the only researcher that has worked out the Tablets of Thoth are talking about the Djinn when they say darkness or night.

Here are some passages from the tablet. This first text is referring to the light energy beings, the ones that join with us.

"Now I depart from ye. Know my commandments, keep them and be them, and I will be with you, helping and guiding you into the light."

You would have noticed the word light. They are not talking about sunlight. They are talking about themselves. A light energy being. Now we can break down some passages where they talk about another entity.

"Deep in the halls of life grew a flower, flaming, expanding, driving back with the night. Placed in the centre, a ray of great potence, life giving, light giving, filling with, power all who came near it." The part when it says driving back the night, it is not referring to night time, it is actually talking about the Djinn. Remember translations back then did not have the word Djinn; that word came way way later.

This next passage shows to me that the Djinn do possess humans, as in, take over their mind, just as we have possessions today and an exorcist would have to remove the Djinn:

"He who by progress has grown from the darkness, lifted himself from the night into light, free is he made of the halls of Amenti, free of the flower of light and of life.

Guided he then, by wisdom and knowledge, passes from man, to the master of life.
There he may dwell as one with the masters, free from the bonds of the darkness of night."

On its own that passage might not make you think the night or darkness is another entity, but I will say a few more passages now.
"Before me arose a great throne of darkness, veiled on its seated a figure of night. Darker than darkness sat the great figure, dark with the darkness not of the night. Before, it then paused the master, speaking the word that brings about life, saying, 'Oh, master, of darkness, guide of the way from life unto life, before the eye bring a son of the morning.

Touch him not ever with the power of night. Call not his flame to the darkness of night. Know him and see him, one of our brothers, lifted from darkness into the light. Release thou his flame from its bondage, free let it flame through the darkness of night.'"

And now here is another passage.
"Then in the midst of the flames in the darkness grew there one that drove forth the night, flaming, expanding, ever brighter, until at last was nothing but light." Then spoke. "My guide, the voice of the master, see your own soul as it grows in the light, free now, forever from the Lord of the night."

And here is one more passage.
"There are plenty, but I hope by now you are starting to see like I did, the night is an entity.

Down I knelt before that great wisdom, feeling the light flowing through me in, waves.
Had I then the voice of the dweller, zero darkness, come into the light. Long. Have you sought the pathway to the light? Each soul on earth that loosens its fetters shall, soon be made free from the bondage of night."

Other than the Emerald Tablets of Thoth, where else mentions the Djinn. Djinn, floral Djinn, also called Djinn, Arabic Djinn, in Arabic mythology, a spirit inhabiting the earth but unseen by humans, capable of assuming various forms and exercising extraordinary powers.

The belief in Djinn was common in pre-Islamic Arabia, where they were thought to inspire poets and sutheirs. Djinn, also Romanised as Djinn, with the broader meaning of spirit or demon, depending on sources. Since Djinn are neither innately evil nor innately good, Islam acknowledged spirits from other religions and was able to adapt spirits from other religions during its expansion.

Djinn are not a strictly Islamic concept; they may represent several pagan beliefs integrated into Islam. To assert a strict monotheism and the Islamic concept of torid, Islam denies all affinities between the Djinn and God; this is what I was just saying. Islam understands Djinn are not connected to the Anunnaki.

I am going to read out a passage from Wikipedia; in my view the only part they get right is the possession; here is the Wikipedia text.

Although generally invisible, Djinn are supposed to be composed of thin and subtle bodies; add JSA with Makonem, they can change at will.

They would favour the form of snakes, but also appear as scorpions, lizards or as humans. They even might engage in sexual affairs with humans and produce offspring. If they get hurt by someone, they usually seek out revenge or possess the assailant's body, calling for an exorcism.
Usually the Djinn do not interfere with humans, but live in their own societies structured as tribes, similar to those of pre-Islamic Arabian tribal system.

The reason why I say other than possession is utter rubbish, is because there is no way a human would know if a snake or scorpion or even another human is a Djinn, so in the olden times, if an animal seemed to be behaving unusual then people would say it is a Djinn. When really is it not?

Individual Djinn appear on charms and talismans. They are called upon for protection or magical aid, often under the leadership of a king. Many people who believe in Djinn wear amulets to protect themselves against the assaults of Djinn, sent out by sorcerers and witches.

While some Muslim scholars in the past had ambivalent attitudes towards sorcery, believing that good Djinn do not require one to commit sin, most contemporary Muslim scholars associate dealing with Djinn with idolatry.

It is interesting that people ask Djinn for help, because the Emerald Tablets of Thoth say this.

"Hark ye, O man, to the wisdom of magic. Hark to the knowledge of powers forgotten. Long, long ago in the days of the first man, warfare began between darkness and light. Men, then as now, were filled with both darkness and light, and while in some darkness.

Hell's sway, in others light filled the soul. Aye, age old is this warfare, the eternal struggle between darkness and light. Fiercely, is it fought all through the ages, using strange powers hidden to man?"

The dark and light energy beings are the only ones I know of. Let us look at more modern stories about the Djinn. Djinn are often believed to be able to take control over a human's body.

Although this is a strong belief among many Muslims, some authors argue that since the Qur'an does not explicitly attribute possession to the Djinn, it derives from pre-Islamic beliefs. Morocco, especially, has many possession traditions, including exorcism rituals; however, Djinn cannot enter a person whenever the Djinn wants; rather, the victim must be predisposed for possession in a state of daifa, Arabic, weakness. Feelings of insecurity, mental instability, unhappy love and depression, being tired from the soul, are forms of daifa.

This is exactly the same as the research I have done. I have spoken to many mediums, spiritualists and clairvoyants. The information I gained showed me the Djinn attach themselves to people who are in a weak mental state.

They then attach the person's chakra, breaking it down until it can push out a possible move in with the light energy being that may already be inside the person's pineal gland.

Most exorcists will call up their own spirit guides, light energy beings, before going into the house with the possessed person; then the exorcist will go in the house and their own guardian spirits will attack the Djinn inside the mind of the person possessed.

A Djinn is best known for attaching itself to humans but also inanimate objects; that is where the story of the Djinn and the lamp comes from.

The original Aladdin. The tale of Aladdin is found in the Arabian Nights tales or 1001 Nights.
An enchanting and magical collection of fairy tales of Middle Eastern origin. The Arabian Nights stories were first introduced to Europe in a French translation by Antoine Galland in 1704. The original story of Aladdin is, maybe surprisingly, set in China.

In the earliest versions of the story, Aladdin is Chinese. He is also not an orphaned street urchin but a lazy boy living at home with his mother. All the characters in the tale are also Chinese apart from the wicked magician who is from North Africa. Some scenes of the story take place in North Africa, but we remain in China for the majority of the story.

Agrabah, the city of mystery and enchantment is, in fact, a fictional city imagined for Disney's Aladdin film, 1992. The creators drew inspiration from the city of Baghdad in Iraq and then gave the city a fictional name. Disney also drew on the Indian city of Agra's Taj Mahal for the setting of the story's royal palace.
So if you have a doll and it starts to move, it is not a human spirit, light energy being, it would be a Djinn.

Humans do not have their own soul or light energy being. Humans do not create one. Humans are joined by one that has been here for eternity. To explain why we do not create our own soul or light energy being, we need to first look at the situation as a whole.

We will first look at it as if we do create our own soul or light energy being. We shall pretend we do, to see what would happen. All evidence points to a soul or light energy being joining with a fetus in the mother's womb. Let us pretend this baby has formed its own soul. I will call it soul from now on, but we are talking about the light energy being.

This baby now has a soul, and as the baby grows the soul is part of the baby. Let us pretend that the brain and soul are as one. As the time goes on, the person and soul are one, but there will come a time that the soul will leave the body. As a person dies the soul would leave the body; the soul would be like energy but still retains the person's consciousness.

We now have a ghost. At some point that ghost will move on; every good medium or spiritualist will tell you the ghosts will move up to the next plane of existence. From the next plane, the ghost will then join with another human. We know this because of the proper scientific studies done on reincarnation.

If you search reincarnation studies you will see mainstream science has agreed it is real. Ian Stevenson has studied 2500 cases in 40 years. From those 2500 he could prove that 1200 of them were 100% genuine. By actually finding records of the previous person; I will cover this later in much more detail. But for now our person's soul has now joined with a fetus, so that in the future the fetus will grow up and can have some memories of the previous person's life.

But if the first person's soul has joined with the second fetus, then the second fetus now has two souls inside it. This would repeat over and over to a point in the future where a fetus would have its own soul but also 100 other souls. We know this is not the case as mediums, spiritualists and clairvoyants only ever tell of one soul that leaves the person's body.

We can say that we do not create our own soul. I know some people want to believe it is our own soul, and that after death we are alive again on the other side.
Technically we are alive for a time, but when the time comes to cross over to the next plane of existence then the light energy being takes back control; then that being will have yet another memory of a person inside it.

This explains why people feel that have had multiple lives when really it was the light being that has joined with many people. What is the point of a light being joining with us and then moving on to different people and animals and aliens over and over?

Dolores Cannon who was a regressive hypnotherapist and psychic researcher who records lost knowledge claims that the soul is here to learn, gain wisdom. Dolores is not the only one to say that; in fact any good medium, spiritualist or clairvoyant will tell you the same.

Even people that are with hypnotherapists will say their soul is here to learn. The Emerald Tablets of Thoth state this over and over, that the eternal light energy beings are always trying to gain wisdom.

Here is just one passage from the Emerald Tablets of Thoth.
"Death is followed by immediate rebirth in one of the 31 planes of existence. However in esoteric cosmology, a plane is conceived as a subtle state, level, or region of reality, each plane corresponding to some type, kind, or category of being."

There are some people that believe there is only 7 planes of existence and here are their explanations of the 7th.

The 7th plane of existence:
This is the plane of the creator of all that is, the energy that flows through all things to create life.
Here we have the realisation that we are part of all that is, part of God. On the 7th plane, we can utilise the energies of all the planes without being bound by any oaths and commitments to them. This is because the energy of the 7th plane creates the other planes.
It is the energy that makes the quarks that make the protons, neutrons, and electrons that in turn make up the nucleus of an atom.

The 6th plane of existence:
This is the plane of the laws that create the very fabric of the universe, such as the law of time, the law of magnetism, the law of gravity, the law of light, and many more.

The 5th plane of existence:
This is the plane of the divine and semidivine beings, the plane of the masters, such as Jesus Christ and the Buddha. It is divided into different levels of vibration and consciousness. The lower levels are the ultimate in dualism. Everyone on this planet is some kind of 5th plane being.

The 4th plane of existence:

This plane is the realm of spirit, what some people would call the spirit world. It is where spirits exist after death, where our ancestors are in waiting. It is the school of the 5th plane beings; the spirits of this place are still learning and have not graduated to higher vibrations of reality.

The 3rd plane of existence:
This is the plane of protein-based life forms such as humans and other animals. In part, we have created it so that we can experience the challenge of being governed by emotions and instinctual desires, and the reality of being in a human body in a physical world.
Here we learn how to graduate past the 4th plane and go forward to the 5th plane.

The 2nd plane of existence:
This plane consists of organic material, vitamins, plants, and trees.

The 1st plane of existence:
This plane consists of all the inorganic material on this Earth. The minerals, crystals, soil, and rocks, all the elements that make up the Earth in its raw form, all the atoms in the periodic table before they bind to carbon bases, and so become organic.

Regardless of how many planes of existence, there is agreement that there are different levels.

Personal understanding from talking to a vast number of mediums, spiritualists, and clairvoyants.

1st plane: Here with humans in the 3rd dimension.

2nd plane: Outside the 3rd dimension. It is a state of being where you can see us in the 3rd dimension but we cannot see them. It also has no time. They can move back and forth in time.

They can travel vast distances at the blink of an eye. The 2nd plane is where they can manifest their light energy being shaped as that of a human, a ghost, retaining the human's consciousness.
Their resting state would be an orb. There are old stories which I believe to be true.
They say that once someone who has died has been forgotten, no more friends or relatives to remember them, they can or are forced to cross over to the next plane, which is the 3rd plane.

The 3rd plane is when the human's consciousness is pushed back and the orb takes full control. This is the plane where the energy being can go back in front of the council of seven. As mentioned before, there the being is offered a new host if they would like to join with it.

The being can see the future of the human it will be joining. If the being believes it will learn a lot from joining with that fetus then it will. If not, it will be offered another human or animal etc. to join with. I will explain later what happens if the person dies before the soul has learned all it should. That is when people have near-death experiences. I will talk more about this later.

The 4th plane of existence that I believe is out there is where the souls that have learned enough get moved up to. Only if you have learned enough can you move up. This is where those that have progressed become your spirit guide. Not a guardian angel.

There is no such thing as an angel. The translation really should be an Anunnaki messenger. In fact, angel in Hebrew means messenger.

If you read the ancient texts and not the Bible, you will see angels were flesh and blood and archangels were leaders or pilots as they seem to take people to heaven and back. But of course you cannot return from heaven alive, yet they did. Heaven in ancient texts that predate the Bible means space. Next time you read the Bible or ancient texts change these words and everything will make more sense.
Heaven equals space. Angel equals Anunnaki, alien.

Archangel equals pilot. Firmament equals atmosphere. Gods equals Elohim. Back to the spirit guardians; they can help you, but really they are not helping you. They are helping the light energy being connected to you, but in turn it helps you.

Some people have been helped; they might hear a voice telling them to stop before walking in a road and nearly getting hit. Or they may see a hand turn their steering wheel just in time to save that person from a fatal crash.

The problem is the first thing people say is God saved me or my guardian angel saved me; no one ever says their spirit guide saves them. Well, in fact, some people do say that. In Native American language a totem is a symbol that can represent a tribe, family or an individual.

Traditionally, each individual is assigned nine different animals through their life, with each animal appearing in your life when that lesson is ready to be learned. They are known as animal guides, and the natives believe there is one totem animal that stays with you throughout your life's journey both in the physical and spiritual world.
Your totem animal is known as your guardian spirit. The Native Indians know that it is not angels but spirits, which are the light energy beings.

Next time you feel you had a divine encounter, do not just blindly say thank God or your guardian angel helped you; think logically, it was your spirit guide.
A spirit guide could be a light energy being that has no connection to you, or it may have one someone who knows memory inside it and it feels the need to help you. You can have many spirit guides, and some may be from your soul group. A soul family is comprised of a group of people that your soul energetically resonates with on a mental, emotional, physical and spiritual level.

Sometimes I will refer to soul, but really we are talking light energy beings. Another name for soul family is twin flames. These people are members of the same spirit family as you and they share an intensely strong bond that transcends time and space itself.

When I say family, I mean family that belongs to your light energy being, not your family that you grew up with. Each light energy being can split into more than just itself. I have counted at least six soul mates that people can have, whereas other researchers have said twenty can be in that soul group. We do not know the true amount, but we do know they come from the same light energy being. The light energy being itself is connected to everything.

Think of everything as water. One drop of water is a light energy being; it is connected to the main water even if it leaves it; that same drop of water can split into multiple light energy beings which form the soul group. I know people have said soul mate, as in the one true love, but this is not the case.

A light energy being that is connected to others will try to be part of the family, meaning as one of the light energy beings enters a human in the womb, the others in the soul group might be inside a friend that person meets in their lifetimes. Another could be inside the mum, a boss, a girlfriend, a boyfriend, anyone that would be connected to each other in some way.
This is so they can all learn; next time round, reincarnation, they might swap and know the light energy being is inside a daughter and another is inside the dad and so on. If one of the human hosts dies before the others, that light energy being will either wait around here as a ghost or on the second plane of existence.

It might not need to wait long as it may join with a fetus that will grow up to be a parent; by the time the human has its own child, the other soul group orbs might have had their hosts die and can then join with the parent's new baby fetus. This repeats over and over and over.

Intuitively, most people tend to describe this connection as sharing the same frequency or vibration because of the deep harmony felt. Such a deep and harmonious connection goes beyond sharing the same surface-based personality tastes, hobbies, and opinions. It is an intense magnetic and spiritual bond that is inexplicable to the mind.

Therefore, your soul family is often described as being comprised of souls that are cut from the same energetic cloth as you. Often through past life regression or the life between life sessions people have been able to recognise different people in different lifetimes as current partners, siblings, children in this lifetimes, and recognise they are a part of their soul group.

If you ever crossed paths with someone and felt like you have known them forever, you have; they belong to your soul group.
Even though you have not met in the human world, your soul must have met in the non-physical world. It is possible that you might be friends for the time that you existed without the human form. There is an idea that you have a karmic connection with certain souls.

In the Gujarati language, it is called *"Lainu"*, the link with another soul that causes you to keep crossing paths, positively impacting each other. It describes someone who helps you lead a life that serves a higher purpose. Buddhists believe that we are reborn an infinite number of times, and that relationships can carry over from one lifetime to the next. In each, we have had parents, siblings, partners, teachers, students.

The closest word for it is *"Pratītyasamutpāda"*, the idea that all beings are interrelated. Often someone walks into the room and we feel like we have known them forever. And it may be that we have. In Judaism, your *"Bashert"*, a Yiddish word that roughly translates to *"bestowed"*, is your destined partner. But I also like the Jewish notion of a *"Havruta"*, or learning partner.

That is the person who pushes and challenges you. It is not about finding someone who completes you; it is about finding someone who gives you the opportunity to complete yourself. Dolores Cannon, a regressive hypnotherapist and psychic researcher, talks about soul groups. I use Dolores as a reference because I believe she is spot on when it comes to spirits, afterlife and hypnotherapy.

But I do not believe she has any true knowledge of aliens; the things she has said about aliens are easily proven wrong. A lot. But of course while on TV you cannot look stupid and say you do not know; both Dolores and Sylvia were experts in their field, so if they got asked a question that was outside their field, they still had to answer.

Here is what mediums say about the afterlife, the life where your memories and personality are joined with the light energy being but you are in control.

Until it is time to cross over to the next plane. Your aura is an electromagnetic frequency that surrounds your body. It can be seen, but it can also be felt.

When someone says they are getting a bad vibe, they mean they are somehow connecting to another person's aura and picking up on his or her frequency. Psychic protection is a way of holding your energy and retaining it as your own. When someone crosses over, they see the world through a new perspective.

Each lifetime in the physical plane, if lived correctly, leaves the soul enlightened. When we go to the other side, we become enlightened, especially through the process of reviewing our lives here on Earth. If you passed your beloved grandmother on the street, would not you stop and say hi? Even though they are in another dimension, they still experience, know, and understand the world we live in, and they love us and want us to know this.

So look for signs from them. Once again the University of Virginia has done studies, this time on mediums; you can read their paper online. So what makes a medium special? Why cannot everyone talk to the dead? Mohammed Iqbal wrote this piece
The Third Eye Connection for the Hindu.com.

"Pineal gland, being the only singular structure in the brain and having a strategic position between the two halves, is believed to connect between intellect and the body. This third eye could be activated to spiritual world frequencies, enabling a person to have the sense of all knowing, God-like euphoria and want us all around him," says Dr. Panagaria.

As you can see we are back to the pineal gland, exactly where I say the light energy being connects to a fetus. But it is not just one article that suggests the pineal gland is the way the mediums communicate with the spirits.

There is a book called The Pineal Gland by Marie Silva. The Pineal Gland: Awakening the Third Eye Chakra and Developing Psychic Abilities such as Clairvoyance and Other Types of Intuition, hardback. Even Christiane Northrup MD has said this about the pineal gland.

The pineal gland regulates your body's circadian rhythm daily and seasonally. Pinealocytes, cells that make up the pineal gland, produce and regulate the secretion of melatonin. Serotonin is the precursor of melatonin. Serotonin is acetylated and methylated to yield melatonin within the pineal gland. Melatonin is an indole analog and plays a vital role in circadian rhythm.

It is the regulator of your sleep-wake cycles, menstrual cycle and pituitary gland functions. Melatonin also influences the secretion of neurotransmitters, endorphins and hormones like estrogen, progesterone and DHEA.
Melatonin is associated with bone metabolism, weight loss and cardiovascular health. It also acts as a powerful antioxidant by scavenging free radicals, immunomodulator and anticancer agent.

She has also explained how we can all detox the pineal gland. Detoxifying your pineal gland is not difficult. There are a number of holistic treatments you can try in addition to diet and lifestyle changes. Here are some of the ways you can detox your pineal gland and improve your health.

1. Avoid fluoride. Tap water and toothpaste are the two most common sources of fluoride exposure. Drink pure water to stay hydrated. Spring water is best. You can also try a water filter, but be sure to do your research, because not all water filtration systems filter out fluoride. Use a fluoride-free toothpaste. There are plenty of fluoride-free toothpastes on the market today.
2. Clean up your diet. Eat lots of organic fruits and vegetables and lean protein. You may also want to limit shellfish and tuna if you eat a lot of it, due to the mercury content. Be sure to limit alcohol or stop drinking altogether.
3. Eat foods high in chlorophyll. Dark, leafy greens are a great source of chlorophyll. Wheatgrass, blue-green algae, and chlorella are also great for detoxifying the pineal gland and especially help to rid the body of fluoride.

After Life: Where Does the Spirit Go Once You Die and Before It Reincarnates?

Let us look at religious versions and then after eac
h of their versions I will tell you what I believe happens.

This is from the Church of Jesus Christ. Even though our body dies, our spirit goes to the spirit world. The spirit world is a waiting period until we receive the gift of resurrection, when our spirits will reunite with our bodies.

Our future resurrected body cannot die and will be perfect, free from pain, sickness, and imperfections. It is because of the infinite love of Jesus Christ that everyone will be resurrected. It is at the time of resurrection that each of us will be judged individually by Jesus, our Saviour.

This judgment will be based on our desires, actions, and choices. Only God and Jesus know our hearts and our life circumstances perfectly, so only they can judge us perfectly. This judgment will be one of mercy, healing, and love. See Revelation 21:4. God's ultimate goal is to help all his children return to live with him in the celestial kingdom.

Yet it is our choices here and now that will shape where we spend eternity. We must believe in Jesus Christ, repent of our sins, be baptised in his name, and receive the gift of the Holy Spirit. Let us break this down. The spirit world is a waiting period until we receive the gift of resurrection. But this part is just plain illogical. Our future resurrected body cannot die and will be perfect, free from pain, sickness, and imperfections.

It is because of the infinite love of Jesus Christ that everyone will be resurrected. It is at the time of resurrection that each of us will be judged individually by Jesus, our Saviour. It is illogical because it says when we reincarnate we will be free of pain.

This silly comment assumes that we right now have not already been reincarnated. And if you have been reading this, you will know that the spirit, orb, has reincarnated over and over, yet we feel pain.

We can also dismiss this part. It is because of the infinite love of Jesus Christ that everyone will be resurrected. That is because we have texts from thousands of years before Jesus was born talking about reincarnation.
Which means it is not the infinite love of Jesus Christ that everyone will be resurrected. This next part is about what the Catholic Church believes.

I will break it down after. Individual judgment, sometimes called particular judgment, happens at the moment of death when each individual will be judged on how they have lived their life. The soul will then go to heaven, hell, or purgatory depending on whether their actions have been judged as being in accordance with God's teachings or not.

The part where it says the soul will then go to heaven, we know is wrong, because the ancient text clearly state over and over, that heaven is space. Where they talk about stars in heaven we can see stars, but cannot see heaven.

This part of Catholic text is really, really dumb. Depending on whether their actions have been judged as being in accordance with God's teachings or not.
The reason why it is so dumb is because in order for a person to know God's teachings, the only way would be the Bible, yet the Bible contradicts itself all the time, thus anyone trying to follow the Bible would be doomed to fail.

This next part is from Buddhists.
For most Buddhists, the belief about where you go when you die is not that you go somewhere else, but rather that you are reborn as something and someone completely different.
The idea of rebirth has been around for a very long time, since pre-Buddhist times. It was taken on board by the Buddha, and the idea of a cycle of birth and rebirth became part of his teachings. Buddhists believe that how you behave in this life gives conditions for your later lives.

It is important to remember though how Buddhists believe it is not you that is reborn. It is something else, another entity, another essence, which is dependent on your behaviour. For many Buddhists, death is not seen as an end, but rather a continuation.
We believe you go from life to life, so this can help Buddhists move away from a fear of death, and instead see it as just another part of their journey which they must take. We also make an effort to make death as painless as possible, both for ourselves and our family members, as this will be part of the behaviour I mentioned which will impact your next life.

This means Buddhists often want to ensure their affairs are in order and that their families are cared for before they die, as they know that in their next life they will not be able to do this.
I believe this part is correct rather that you are reborn as something and someone completely different.
This part does not make sense: we believe you go from life to life.
The reason it does not make sense is because it assumes that the very first humans to be born were the ones with a soul, so at some point souls would have had to stop being formed inside humans, so that the soul from another previous person would be able to join with that new person.

Now that we have billions of humans, there was not billions to start with, so what is the limit before humans stopped getting their own soul and started to get a reincarnated one?

It just does not make sense, but an entity like I have said that joins with a human then leaves makes so much more sense. This next part is what the Muslims believe. After death, most Muslims believe that the soul will enter Barzakh, a state of waiting, until the day of judgement. When a person dies, their soul is taken by an angel of death.
God sends two angels to question the waiting soul. The part about the soul being taken does not work as mediums would have told us this, but they have not.

The question is what does the afterlife look like?

According to all good mediums, past life regression and NDE experiences, life after death means, as a spirit, human joined with an orb. You can see everything, all around, up down, to the sides, even through objects. You can hear humans' thoughts.
You can see in bright colours that we cannot see; think of it like ultraviolet and other colours that go beyond humans' range. You live here, or there; you can travel anywhere within a blink of an eye; all you do is think and you will be there.
Even to other planets, you can interact with physical objects; you can sit in a chair made by humans, you can push objects, although this is hard to do and requires a lot of energy.

You can retain your human form or become the shape of the orb. You can manifest objects such as a football, so as a spirit you can kick the ball. You can interact with other spirits, although I have never heard of any fighting. You can see the future and the past.

You cannot give dates as you are not aware of dates anymore, because today could be yesterday if you wanted it to; then as time moves on, you lose the notion of time. You can see pets or some animals when they have passed on. You can dance, sing, walk, fly and be sad, happy and to some degree angry. You cannot kill a human; you cannot tell a human things about the universe or about a source or creation, we call that God.

You can communicate with a loved one while they are still alive, either through mediums or moving, banging things or giving thoughts into the person's dreams. Remember, because you can see the future, you can see how your loved ones will die, from every angle; this is not something I want to see. And because of this I hope there is a way to go directly to the next plane of existence and not stay around here.

How to contact spirits: When I say spirit, I am talking about a person that has died and not yet crossed over to the second plane. Never attempt to communicate with spirits alone as you can bring them through and they may not leave. Firstly from my own experience using a makeshift Ouija board and asking the spirit if it can read my mind, the answer was yes. I then asked the spirit a few questions in my mind, and the glass went to the answers each time.

This proves to me spirits are real and can read our thoughts, which makes sense if you have been watching what I have said about the pineal gland being a receiver and transmitter. With that in mind, let us look at the options to tell a spirit something. At the end of the options I will give solutions on how to understand a spirit's reply.

1. Thought
2. A medium or clairvoyant etc. If they say the word angels or heaven, avoid. Watch my other videos on my website. ourtruehistory.co.uk
3. A spirit box
4. Dousing rods
5. EMF radars
6. Be a channel for them
7. Use a Ouija board
8. Automatic writing
9. Use a camera.

Let us look at the first one, thought. Anyone at any time can think of a loved one or someone you know that has passed. If they have not gone to plane 2, they will hear your thoughts, but how?

Everything is connected; the spirit, orb, that is inside you can connect to any orb; it does not have to be part of the soul group. It seems to work on the quantum level. But what then? So you have put a thought out there, but how do you get a reply? For spirits to reply, it is better at the darkest time, when the sun is on the other side.

For some reason spirits struggle with the white light frequency; that is why in séances they used only a red light bulb. Ask the spirit to knock something over, tap on a door, touch your shoulder, make a noise.

Or you can put two glasses almost touching, both with tiny amounts of water. Ask the spirit to push one of them, so that you hear a ting sound. Use TE-1 for yes method and 2 for no, to get your answers.

Mediums

Today, psychic entities can be seen in magazine ads, television ads, and throughout the internet, but how do you know who is the best one?

Truth be told, you can spend countless hours going to each one, or you can take these tips to help you find the best psychic reader. Ask around.

There was once a time where going to a psychic for advice was seen as taboo. However, in today's world, with so many questions surrounding day to day living, psychics are seeing a resurgence in new clients. No longer are these individuals surrounded by negative connotations and those that have seen psychics in the past are happy to talk about their experiences.

Asking around to friends and family is among the best way to find your ideal psychic reader. You will find that many of the people closest to you likely visit their psychic on a regular basis, so take advice from those who have avidly sought help from a psychic. Know what you are looking for.

Like all people, psychics have their strengths and weaknesses.

Not all are exactly the same and it pays to understand what you want in your chosen psychic. Your psychic might be clairvoyant, be able to channel spirits, perform an aura reading, or a myriad of other psychic attributes.

Before settling on a psychic, understand your needs and how that person may help you connect with your future, past, and present ideally.

The possibilities are endless with the variety of psychics available these days, so think carefully about the spiritual reader you choose. Read reviews. Like all businesses these days, psychics can be reviewed.

As online reviews have become a highly credible source of information these days, it pays to check out a psychic's online reviews before scheduling a reading. Be careful on certain review sites and keep in mind that just because a psychic may have one or two bad reviews does not mean they are not good at what they do.

Negative reviews can be an indicator of a bad psychic if they are abundantly available, but more often than not, a few bad reviews are just from angry customers not happy with the information received from their psychic.

There are also plenty of online trolls that never went to the individual, but are simply out to mar their reputation for the sake of being mean, so keep that in mind as well. Check their social media. Finding the best psychic does not mean you have to try out each one, but simply be crafty in how you interview them.

Social media sites are the way most psychics advertise and reach out to clients these days and just like any other social media site, it will tell you a lot about the individual. The psychic will have much more than just there, about information available through past posts, videos, and even live sessions with real clients.

Take your time to research by combing through their past posts and discover a little more about how that particular psychic works. Watch out for outlandish promises.

True psychics believe in their abilities and do not have to promise their clients the world in order to make a living. It is not about money with a true psychic and you will not feel bullied into having a session with them.

A Spirit Box

What is a spirit box? A spirit, ghost, or Frank's box is a device that quickly jumps through AM radio channels, creating a white noise effect. That effect allows spirits or ghosts to communicate by altering energy to create words and phrases.

It is said that clear phrases and responses can be heard while sometimes even intelligent responses can be made out.
The spirit box was created in 2002 by Frank Sumption, thus the name Frank's box. Frank made a total of 180 boxes and distributed them to whoever he saw fit to hear the voice. Today there are only 97 originals in existence.

So how do you use a spirit box? It is as easy as turning it on and allowing it to skip through the radio stations; you can play around with it and get used to how it sounds and feels. After a while you may hear little sounds and different words but do not be discouraged if you cannot make out sentences or responses.

Seasoned ghost hunters will tell you it took lots and lots of tries before they were able to effectively communicate.

Dousing Rods
What are dousing rods?

Dousing rods are rods or sticks traditionally shaped in an L used to find anything from water, jewels, dead bodies, and in our case communicate with unfound ghosts.

The word dousing means a technique for searching for underground water, minerals, or anything invisible by observing the motion of a pointer, traditionally a forked stick, now often paired bent wires, or the changes in direction of a pendulum, supposedly in response to unseen influences.

Your rods will react to the energy in the environment and the energy you are giving off, allowing them to reflect and guide you to something or answer questions. So how do you use a dousing rod?

Hold one in each hand and take a deep breath. The best way to start is by asking permission, *"May I start dousing?"* and then asking questions you know the answer to.

Get accustomed to how the rods feel and how they move or respond to questions. Then go find some ghosts.

EMF Radars

What are EMF radars? EMF radars are most often used to find faults in electrical wiring and power lines. An EMF radar will find moving electrical charges and the magnetic field created by said charges.

The cool thing is it can differentiate moving between stationary so it will avoid picking up things like the Earth's magnetic field. So how do you use an EMF radar?

Walk around and wait for the machine to read spikes in energy. Once you have been using the box for a while it may even respond to questions.

But careful for false readings; the machine could pick up things like your cell phone so it is wise to get accustomed to the box to make sure you are using it to its maximum potential before asking questions.

The best way to use these special machines and devices is just to get used to them and use repetition.

Channel a Spirit Yourself

Decide between exploring your consciousness and communing with the spirit world. Different traditions use the word *"channeling"* in different ways. Some channelers aim outward, in an attempt to contact others, or inward, to learn more about the self, too.
Depending on your interests and goals, this decision can lead you into very different traditions, rituals, and practices, though most types of channeling involve a similar process: first inducing of a trance-like state and then communicating with some other.

In supernatural or spirit channeling, the goal is to tap into the world of spirits and communicate with them. Practitioners often want to contact deceased relatives or famous historical figures, or otherwise make some contact with the dead. Spirit channeling as we think of it today, with crystal balls and Ouija boards, was extremely popular in intellectual occult circles in the mid to late 19th century.

Though this kind of for-profit mediumship is widely dismissed by scientific skeptics as an orchestrated con against the often wealthy participants, spirit channeling has historical roots that extend far beyond the Victorian stereotypes.

Consciousness channeling is a newer phenomenon. In some New Age philosophies, practitioners of channeling will meditate and attempt to visualise archetypal figures that are manifestations of their own subconscious, past-life figures, or metaphorical representatives of some psychological trauma.

This figure will often guide the participant through different interactions and communications with the aim of healing the spirit and learning about the self. Be open to wrestling with strange phenomena. Whether you want to find comfort and understanding by consulting an oracle, or you seek a deepened understanding of life and death, it is important to articulate your goals for channeling and be realistic about them.

If you are going to embark on a channeling journey, it is important to commit to an often quizzical, mysterious way of interpreting the messages you receive. The better you are at receiving them, the more you will get out of the experience. Embrace the mystery of it.

Anyone who has ever cracked open an I Ching or tried to learn about tarot knows that channeling can be a frustrating and complex process. It does not always work like a movie, where a candle flickers and you hear the voice of some long-dead relative.

Have a specific inquiry in mind, a specific thing you want to learn, and accept that you might not get the answer you are looking for. Take it seriously. If your goal is to get out a Ouija board and ask a ghost what afterlife farts smell like, you should probably spend your time doing something more constructive.

Channeling only works if the participant is fully committed and open to the possibility of learning something about yourself and consciousness that might be hard to believe or understand.

Read up on occult symbology and symbolism. Because the process often involves the interpretation of symbols, it is important to do a little research before you jump in head first to get more out of the experience.

It is unlikely that any spirit guides, internal or external, will come forth to answer a question that is unserious, dishonest, or trivial, so give some thought to an appropriate question that deserves a complicated answer. Make it specific, but not too specific.

A question like *"Does Bill really hate me when I show up late for work?"* is probably better saved for a Magic 8 Ball.

You want your query to be broad enough to allow for complexity and personal enough to be worthwhile.

"How can I be a better person in my work?" is more like it.

Let one question lead to another. If you are concerned about your work persona, let that question spiral into more questions, so you may look for possible answers in your investigation.

Who am I when I work? What does my work mean to me? How should I approach my work? What is a worker?

These may all be applicable questions that circle around your initial one. Look for the answers to questions you did not ask.

Start keeping a dream journal. As you embark on a journey into your mind, you may find it more and more difficult to distinguish between the dream state and your waking life.

Symbols will surround you and will pop up at unexpected times. This is a good thing. You just need to be ready to capture them for further analysis later, making a dream journal or a channeling journal an excellent resource for your investigation.

Keep a small composition book beside your bed. When you wake from any dream, however boring or uneventful, write down everything you remember from it immediately. What did you see? What did you feel? Who was there?

This kind of interpretation and attention to detail will serve you well in your channeling experiments. Meditate deeply, focusing on your breathing. Find a quiet, meditative location where you will feel comfortable and calm. Settle into a comfortable sitting position on the floor or in a straight-backed chair and sit with your body upright, your back straight. Go with soft, natural lighting and silence. Close your eyes or focus somewhere in the middle distance; a blank wall or a calming spot would do nicely.

Articulate your intentions for this meditation by centering yourself around some mantra like,
"I will achieve trance and I will return to normal consciousness with a full memory of what I experienced. I will achieve a deeper and deeper trance state with practice."

You do not need to sit in the lotus position in the middle of a crossroads at midnight or prostrate yourself in front of a goat skull and candles to channel.

Ouija Board

Use the Ouija board. The Ouija with Ouija, 4 slash deep G, also known as a spirit board or talking board, is a flat board marked with the letters of the Latin alphabet, the numbers 0 to 9, the words yes, no, occasionally hello and goodbye, along with various symbols and graphics.

It uses a planchette, small heart-shaped piece of wood or plastic, as a movable indicator to spell out messages during a séance. Participants place their fingers on the planchette and it is moved about the board to spell out words.

Ouija is a trademark of Hasbro, but is often used generically to refer to any talking board. Spiritualists in the United States believed that the dead were able to contact the living and reportedly used the talking board very similar to a modern Ouija board at their camps in the US state of Ohio in 1886 to ostensibly enable faster communication with spirits.

Automatic Writing

Experiment with automatic writing. For some participants, especially those interested in plumbing the depths of their consciousness, experimenting with automatic writing is an effective way of communicating with the unknown.

Start with your trance meditation and move to writing in response to your queries. All you have got to do is get out a pen and a piece of paper and write unconsciously, without pausing or paying attention to the words you are writing.

This is an excellent way of getting in touch with your own messages and reinforcing the agency and divinity of the self.

You have got your own answers and can get in touch with them via automatic writing. It is also effective to write down all your communications with your spirit guide, after extracting yourself from your trance state.

It is important to keep a record of these communications, to allow yourself to investigate them later for parallels and symbolic echoes.

A Camera

Old photos were said to be able to capture orbs and spirits, more so than using today's digital cameras. But there is a way to see a spirit moving. Some apps on phone or the Xbox Kinect cameras look for a figure; if it sees one it will display it either as stick figure or as an avatar.

Because the video cameras can now see a deeper range of frequencies, many spirits have been seen walking, sitting down and doing normal things a human would do. Of course if you are playing a game using the camera and suddenly another player joins you, and you cannot see them in your room, but they are there; they even sit on your rocking chair and it moves. You might be a little scared.

Go to YouTube and type in Xbox Kinect ghost. Whatever you do to attract a spirit, be respectful, be kind, because one day you will be on the other side, trying desperately to get a message across to the living, just as most of them on the other side are trying to do.

Life Review

An out-of-body experience, OBE or sometimes OOBE, is a phenomenon in which a person perceives the world from a location outside their physical body.

An OBE is a form of autoscopy, literally seeing self, although this term is more commonly used to refer to the pathological condition of seeing a second self, or doppelganger. In simple terms your spirit-like energy being leaves your body, just as if you have died.

My feeling is that the pineal gland is relaxed enough, either due to lack of blood flow, or you are in a state like meditation. Once your pineal gland is able to let the energy being go, you are connected to it, even in control of it, just like you would be when you die. The one thing that everyone says after they wake up is they were snapped back into their body. So why did not these people have a life review?

No they are either sent back to their body by a light being or the doctors wake them up; either way they were not dead. The only way you get a life review is when you die and do not come back. What is a life review?

There are different ways people think of it. Here are some, and then at the end I will tell you my thoughts, which no one else has ever said. The term life review, or flashback before death, refers to a phenomenon widely reported as occurring during near-death experiences, one, in which a person rapidly sees much or the totality of their life history.

Life review is often described by people claiming to have experienced this phenomenon as having their life flash before their eyes. There is evidence that a type of judgment occurs at the time of death. This judgment involves the review of a person's life and results in their placement in the spirit world.

Sometime after the judgment the person is assigned, in many cases this assignment is self-imposed, to a specific place or level in the other world, a place where his or her spirit feels most at ease.

Muslim: Eunice explains that when a Muslim is approaching death, they often reflect on and review their lives and seek God's forgiveness for anything they have done wrong. This is something private between them and God. They do not need to confess to another person, but they will ask forgiveness from God himself without any sort of mediator.

Those around the bed do not need to know what it is that the dying person is seeking God's forgiveness for. Catholic: When we die, or more correctly, fall asleep in the Lord, oneness. For 14, we reverently bury the body of the one who has passed from this life to the next.

While the body is buried, as was the body of the Lord Jesus, the soul goes on to judgment. This judgment is before the Lord and he judges us on our faithfulness to the gospel and the work that follows from that faithfulness. Actually, we judge ourselves by how we lived our lives, how well we tried to conform our lives to the life of Jesus.
Two judgments: The judgment right after death is called the particular judgment. At the time of our falling asleep, we are judged either as worthy of the eternal life of heaven, which may first require a stop-off in a place of purification from any last remaining imperfections, or are separated from God and consigned to eternal life in hell.

This particular judgment awaits all of us at the very moment that we die and it will be clear in an immediate way.

The general judgment is that act of judgment which accompanies the glorious return of Jesus Christ in his second coming, when he comes to judge the living and the dead, as we say in professing the Nicene Creed.

This general judgment is characterised by the Lord's own words in Matthew 25:31–46, as Jesus speaks of how he will separate the sheep from the goats, saying to the sheep at his right that they are to inherit the kingdom, as they fed the hungry, gave drink to the thirsty, etc. He is sending the goats off to eternal punishment for not having carried out the way of charity.

The Catechism of the Catholic Church states that this general judgment will reveal even to its furthest consequences the good each person has done or failed to do during his earthly life. CCC 1039, Everything that was hidden will be revealed to all, the just and the damned.

Our True History's Version of the Life Review

After speaking with many, many mediums and clairvoyants, it has become clear that the Emerald Tablets of Thoth are actually correct.
In the tablets it states this:

"And spirit shall ye reach that halls of Amenti, and bring back the wisdom that liveth in light. Know ye the gateway to power is secret. List to the wisdom that gives thee of death. When at the end of their work appointed, thou may desire to pass from this life. Pass to the plain where the sons of the morning live and have been as children of light. Pass without pain and pass without sorrow. Into the plain where is eternal light."

It clearly shows that the work is wisdom and that once done the light energy being can move up to another plane of existence. Not impossible is it to grow, to a consciousness above.

For when two has become one, and one has become the all, know ye the barrier has lifted, and ye are made free of the road. Grow thou from form to the formless. Free may thou be of the road. Ye, as a child, had not the knowledge. That came to ye when ye became a man. Compare ye the cycles to man in his journey.

From birth unto death. And see in the cycle below thee the child. With the knowledge he has. And see ye yourself as the child grown older. Advancing in knowledge as time passes on. See ye, we, also, the child grown to manhood. With the knowledge and wisdom that came. With the years. So also, O.S.O.F.E. are the cycles of consciousness. Children in different stages of growth.

Yet all from the one source, the wisdom. No, O.N.E. ye should aim at perfection. For only thus can ye attain to the goal. Though ye should know that nothing is perfect. Yet it should be thy aim and thy goal.

If perfection for the spirit, light energy being is the main goal, then a review of the life it spent with you would be logical, to see what it needs to improve for the next time around.
This time in another different person, moving from person to person as each one dies, learning each time for the perfection they need.

It makes sense for a light being to review its own life attached to you.

There is no point in reviewing your life, because when the light energy being crosses over to the next plane, you cease to be.

Looking back at your own life is pointless; even if you did come back in the body of another person, you would need to know what you need to do to improve. Yet people do not even know they have had a previous life, let alone know what to do for this new life.
But an old, light energy being would know and would choose the next person it is going to join with to gain the missing wisdom that it needs.

There seems to be laws on the other side; when a medium asks the spirits a question like, *"Is there a God?"* The spirit replies, *"I cannot answer that."* Is that because they do not know? Or is there a rule they cannot break? *"I believe there are rules."* I also believe there is a deep alien connection with the orbs. Journalist Linda Moulton Howe has said that three different alien races are at war with each other and they steal the orb from each other's bodies.

I have also heard remote viewers say they have seen little grey aliens moving light energy balls around. Alien abductees have said, *"They have seen a human on a table in a spaceship, above the person lying down is a tube and then a light energy ball leaves the body goes up through the tube into a container that has a copy of the person lying there, the light ball goes into that person."*
This would suggest a clone that has now got all the memories of the original.
Another abductee has said they were on a craft and there was rows and rows of cages; inside were light energy balls; the abductee asks what are they?

The grey replied, *"Nothing to do with you."* The question is, are the aliens capturing the light beings and are bad to them, or do they work together?

The Emerald Tablets of Thoth talk about the more evolved light energy beings living inside the Earth. If this is true then that would explain why so many people have seen light energy balls come out from the ground and even form crop circles.

Watch this video I made about it.

I want to show you how media lies and how people that originally tell the truth are persuaded not to tell the truth anymore. Back in 1996 in the UK near Oliver's Castle, a guy was walking his dog, and he had his 8mm tape camera with him. That is not impossible because I used to walk around with my tape camera. He saw these orbs flying around this field while he was walking his dog and he started to record them because he thought that was really weird. They created a crop circle which I will show you in a minute if you have not already seen it. People try and debunk that. I remember the original story.

The original story was that he then went to his local pub and started showing everyone the footage on the camera. They were all shocked and then word spread; local newspaper got involved and then bigger newspapers and then America in fact got involved.

They went to special effects industry people and asked them if this footage is real. The special effects people said yes, they looked over and said yes we believe it is real.

Bear in mind 1996, this was when Windows 95 had just come out.

You were talking about very slow computers.

Jurassic Park was only 3 years before this. For someone to have the ability to do what he had done was remarkable with a Windows 95 computer. Editing software can do it now obviously but back then it could not.

What is interesting is this guy filmed this handheld.
Now I am going to play it. You will see my camera wobbling but he was wobbling as well.
Right so there is the orbs and before you know it these crop circles. This is consistent with loads of other people saying that they have seen orbs create crop circles but obviously he was lucky enough to have his camera on. So it is wobbly; see if the camera worked, there was all over the place.

Now the debunkers on TV shows have turned around and said it was fake because and they recreated it. They locked the camera down. If you know anything about filming, when you lock a camera down you have what they call a clean plate. So there would have been a crop field with no circle in it.
They record for a minute and then they go down, spend 2 and a half hours making the crop circle, come back and press record again. And because the camera is locked in position you can manipulate that. Yes back in '96 you could have done that.

Dissolved from one to the other so it looks like within a few seconds the crop circle was formed. But his was handheld. Match moving software or camera tracking software did not come well into the 2000s. So that is genuine from that point of view.
Now later on people say that he was doing it for media.

Seriously if he was doing some sort of stunt with an 8mm camera the quality was pathetic. So he was persuaded I believe to change his story.

So just carrying on with the view from the video last time. The guy I believe ended up working in graphics or computer editing or special effects.

But obviously he was interested in it otherwise he would not have had an 8mm camera and they were not cheap back then for his age anyway. So he moved into that so then of course the debunkers turned around and said *"Oh well he did that back in '96"*. Does not quite work like that; just because he was interested in filming and everything, does not mean that he did that back in '96 and obviously the technology for Windows 95 did not have the technology that he had there. And as I say experts actually watched it; it was not just a merge; it was the actual crop got flattened in a circular motion.

But there are other footage out there of orbs flying around cornfields so it all makes sense and it is genuine.

Crop circles date back to 1678 and that is just the first recorded evidence.

The Mowing Devil.
A wood carving of a crop circle. The person that carved it could not work out how it was done in the darkness of night and how quick. This was not the first time he had crop circles so he carved a devil doing it.

I have done videos on crop circles and how we can tell what ones are man-made and what are genuine.

I have done videos on crop circles and how to tell. The nodes on the crop are superheated with a type of microwave. The node expands and bursts. This makes the corn stem bend. Man-made crop circles are just flattened with a plank of wood.

Also the orb-created circles produce 400% more yield than the surrounding untouched corn. But what are the crop formations? I hear you ask. We know they are not for humans to read because we mostly need to be at least a thousand foot in the air to see them. We did not have that tech back then.

I believe there are messages for aliens above to see, messages about the planet, giving the aliens details of how planet Earth is doing. This would make sense as people have seen UFOs over crop circles but have never seen a UFO create a crop circle.

If you were a light energy ball, you could not talk but you could manipulate some things, then creating an image or text for aliens to read is logical.
With this in mind it does appear that orbs are in connection with some types of aliens.

Sadly, some religions are aware of orbs, but they call them angel orbs. By calling them angel orbs, this allows them to dismiss aliens, or anything else, except for a religious context.

The question is, are we able to say that life can be energy? We know what we are made from and we also know that on other planets there are other elements that we do not have here on Earth.

First we can see there is life on Earth that actually lives off energy.

We have known bacteria to survive on a variety of energy sources, but none as weird as this. Think of Frankenstein's monster, brought to life by galvanic energy, except these electric bacteria are very real and are popping up all over the place. Unlike any other living thing on Earth, electric bacteria use energy in its purest form, naked electricity in the shape of electrons harvested from rocks and metals.

We already knew about two types, Shewanella and Geobacter. Now, biologists are showing that they can entice many more out of rocks and marine mud by tempting them with a bit of electrical juice. Experiments growing bacteria on battery electrodes demonstrate that these novel, mind-boggling forms of life are essentially eating and excreting electricity.

This leads to the question: what is energy? The law of conservation of energy states that energy can neither be created nor destroyed, only converted from one form of energy to another. This means that a system always has the same amount of energy, unless it is added from the outside.

In 2003 the New Scientist published an article which states, *"Physicists have created blobs of gaseous plasma that can grow, replicate and communicate, fulfilling most of the traditional requirements for biological cells."*

So there we have it: life in the shape of a sphere, orb, that is energy, just like the light energy beings that join with humans, and they also join with aliens.

To sum up everything you need to know about spirits.

Light energy beings were created at the same time as the universe. They cannot die; I am unsure if they can reproduce or create new orbs.

There are at least two types of orbs, both fighting each other since the dawn of time.

One would be called light energy beings, the other called night, or Jinn.

They are bored; bored because living in the universe with nothing to do makes them so bored.
As life started on planets, they took an interest, watched from afar and eventually they worked out how to join with the pineal gland while the host is still in the mother's womb.

This allowed the orbs to learn, learn a different perspective on life. Although 100 years for an orb to be joined with someone is just a blink of an eye for the lifespan it has, it still learns and will go from one person to another, gaining that wisdom they need to move up to the next plane of existence.

Once they get to the next plane of existence they become a guardian, watching over people, making sure the orb inside the person learns as much as it can.

Then when the guardian learns enough about helping and watching, it will move up another plane of existence. At this point there are too many guesses to say what it does; there is no one that can really tell us what happens beyond the guardian plane.

Humans do die; we have a brief moment where we are joined with the orb after death, but at some point the orb takes control and moves up to the next plane, pushing your memories back and is now just a memory of the next person that has that orb can recall a past life, not their life, but another person's life they think was theirs, simply because they have accessed the orb's memory.

It is a sobering thought that while we are dead, for a time we can see forward and backwards in time, we can communicate through mediums to tell our loved ones we are okay.

But the downside to seeing everything is you will be able to see how your loved ones will die; a horrible thought is you may see a loved one murdered and there is nothing you can do. Or is there? We know group manifestations seem to work; that is when we call for help to make it rain or pray for healing.

We could while on the other side, get together as many spirits as you can and use all your energy to push a murderer down the stairs, before the murder even happens.

Our spirits are not allowed to hurt people. We know poltergeists do harm and so do Jinn, but we do not know if they can kill. The good news is that when you die, as long as your loved ones have not already crossed over to the next plane of existence, you will be able to see them in the afterlife.

Chapter 16

Other researchers

For any researcher exploring the connections between Mesopotamian lore (like the Anunnaki traditions) and the Hebrew Bible, Robert William Rogers' Cuneiform Parallels to the Old Testament is an indispensable foundational work.

First published in 1912, this book was a landmark achievement in comparative mythology. Its purpose was clear and revolutionary for its time: to systematically present translated cuneiform texts from Assyria, Babylonia, and Persia that shared striking thematic, narrative, and conceptual parallels with the Old Testament.

Robert William Rogers (1864–1930) was a distinguished American linguist and historian. His expertise in Akkadian, Sumerian, and Hebrew allowed him to act as both translator and compiler. He didn't work in isolation; he collaborated with a network of leading Assyriologists and drew primarily from the vast collections of the British Museum, including the famed library of Ashurbanipal at Nineveh.

Rogers organized his material not as a dry history, but as a thematic anthology. He placed cuneiform inscriptions side-by-side with their potential biblical counterparts, allowing the parallels to speak for themselves. This structure makes it a powerful tool for seeing the shared cultural and literary bedrock of the ancient Near East.
This book provides the primary source evidence that connects these Mesopotamian deities and their stories to the later biblical world.

The major thematic sections covered in the book are a veritable checklist of key comparative topics:

Thematic SectionKey Content & Relevance

1. Mythological TextsThe Creation Epic (Enuma Elish), The Gilgamesh Epic, The Flood Story (Utnapishtim), The Descent of Ishtar, and legends of primordial kings. These are essential for comparing Mesopotamian and biblical cosmogony, heroism, and divine judgment.
2. Hymns & Wisdom LiteraturePrayers to gods like Sin and Ishtar, lamentations, and a "Babylonian Job." Illuminates the shared poetic and philosophical forms between the cultures.
3. Liturgical & Doctrinal TextsDetails on rituals, the pantheon, and a "Babylonian Sabbath." Provides context for the religious and ritualistic milieu that influenced regional practices.
4. Chronological MaterialsKing lists and chronicles that help synchronize Mesopotamian and biblical timelines, anchoring mythical events in a historical framework.
5. Historical TextsAnnals of kings like Sargon II, Sennacherib (who besieged Jerusalem), and Nebuchadnezzar II. These texts often directly corroborate or provide the "other side" of events described in the books of Kings and Chronicles.
6. Legal TextsBusiness documents, omens, and the crown jewel: The Code of Hammurabi. Crucial for understanding the legal and social context that underpins Mosaic Law.

Rogers was careful not to claim simple "borrowing." Instead, he presented these texts as evidence of a common "milieu of ideas" from which both Mesopotamian and Israelite traditions emerged.

His work allows us to see the Hebrew Bible not in isolation, but as a profound document that engaged with, challenged, and refined the dominant narratives of its time.

Over the past 150 years, a range of scholars—ranging from pioneering Assyriologists to contemporary biblical historians—have examined the deep connections between Mesopotamian literature and the Hebrew Bible. Their work reveals not simple copying, but a complex process of cultural adaptation, theological reinterpretation, and literary transformation.

These early researchers laid the groundwork as cuneiform tablets were first deciphered and published.

George Smith (1840–1876)
A self-taught Assyriologist at the British Museum, Smith made a landmark discovery in 1872 while studying tablets from the library of Ashurbanipal.

He identified the Babylonian Flood narrative within the *EPIC OF GILGAMESH,* a story strikingly similar to the biblical account of Noah.

His public announcement sent shockwaves through Victorian intellectual circles and marked the first clear evidence that key biblical stories had older Mesopotamian antecedents.

Friedrich Delitzsch (1850–1922)
A leading German Assyriologist, Delitzsch ignited fierce controversy with his lecture series *BABEL UND BIBEL* ("Babel and Bible").

He argued aggressively that the Bible was not only later in date but deeply indebted to Babylonian religious and legal traditions, challenging notions of its divine uniqueness. Though his rhetoric was often polemical (and later tainted by anti-Semitic overtones), his work forced a necessary reckoning with the Bible's ancient Near Eastern context.

Hermann Gunkel (1862–1932)
A pioneer of form criticism, Gunkel demonstrated in works like *SCHÖPFUNG UND CHAOS* that the Genesis creation accounts drew upon much older mythological motifs, particularly the cosmic battle against the sea dragon (Tiamat in the *ENUMA ELISH*; Leviathan or Rahab in the Bible).

He showed how Israelite scribes repurposed these myths to serve a monotheistic worldview.

Contemporary researchers no longer ask *WHETHER* the Bible borrowed from older traditions, but *HOW* and *WHY*.

Their focus is on the sophisticated theological reworking of shared cultural material.

The Biblical Archaeology School
William F. Albright (1891–1971) and his students sought to anchor the Bible in historical reality. While often defending its reliability, they also documented extensive parallels between Israelite and Mesopotamian law, ritual, and narrative, helping establish the Bible as a product of its ancient world.

Comparative Mythologists and Ancient Near Eastern Specialists

Thorkild Jacobsen (1904–1993): In *THE TREASURES OF DARKNESS*, he traced the evolution of Mesopotamian religion with poetic insight, providing essential context for understanding biblical theology.

Alexander Heidel (1907–1955): His accessible studies—*THE BABYLONIAN GENESIS* and *THE GILGAMESH EPIC AND OLD TESTAMENT PARALLELS,* remain classics for their clear, systematic comparison of texts.

Michael Coogan: Through works like *THE OLD TESTAMENT: A HISTORICAL AND LITERARY INTRODUCTION*, he emphasizes how biblical authors participated in a shared literary and legal culture across the ancient Near East.

Peter Machinist: His research on Assyrian-Israelite interactions reveals how biblical writers consciously engaged with—and resisted—imperial ideologies.

Karen R. Nemet-Nejat: In *DAILY LIFE IN ANCIENT MESOPOTAMIA,* she reconstructs the social and intellectual world in which these stories lived, showing how myth and law formed the "mental furniture" of the region.

Irving Finkel: A current curator at the British Museum, Finkel's discovery and translation of a cuneiform tablet describing a *ROUND ARK* in *THE ARK BEFORE NOAH* renewed public interest in the Mesopotamian roots of the Flood story.

Scholars of Israelite Religion

Mark S. Smith (NYU): In *THE EARLY HISTORY OF GOD* and *THE ORIGINS OF BIBLICAL MONOTHEISM*, he traces how Yahweh gradually absorbed traits of older Canaanite deities like El and Baal, evolving from a national god into the sole deity of monotheism.

John Day (Oxford): His detailed studies—*YAHWEH AND THE GODS AND GODDESSES OF CANAAN* and *GOD'S CONFLICT WITH THE DRAGON AND THE SEA*—show how biblical poets deliberately reinterpreted Canaanite and Mesopotamian myths to affirm Israel's unique covenant with God.

In contrast to academic scholarship stands the work of **Zecharia Sitchin (1920–2010)**, whose *EARTH CHRONICLES* series proposed that ancient Sumerian texts described visits by extraterrestrials, the Anunnaki, from a planet called Nibiru. According to Sitchin, these beings genetically engineered humanity and founded civilization.

While Sitchin claimed to base his theories on direct translations of cuneiform tablets, the vast majority of those texts had already been published and translated by professional Assyriologists, beginning with George Smith in the 1870s and continuing through scholars like Samuel Noah Kramer and Thorkild Jacobsen. Sitchin did not work from unpublished or newly discovered material; rather, he offered highly selective and unconventional readings of existing translations.

This is why when you hear people say Sitchins translations are wrong, laugh at them, because he didn't translate, they were mostly done before he was born!

He could translate, but they had already been translated.

His major works include:

The Earth Chronicles Series:

1. *THE 12TH PLANET* (1976)
2. *THE STAIRWAY TO HEAVEN* (1980)
3. *THE WARS OF GODS AND MEN* (1985)
4. *THE LOST REALMS* (1990)
5. *WHEN TIME BEGAN* (1993)
6. *THE COSMIC CODE* (1998)
7. *THE END OF DAYS* (2007)

Companion Works:
8. *GENESIS REVISITED* (1990)
9. *DIVINE ENCOUNTERS* (1995)
10. *THE EARTH CHRONICLES EXPEDITIONS* (2004)
11. *THE EARTH CHRONICLES HANDBOOK* (2009)
12. *THERE WERE GIANTS UPON THE EARTH* (2010, posthumous)
13. *THE ANUNNAKI CHRONICLES* (2015, compiled posthumously)

Chapter 17

Lesser Gods / The Igigi

There is growing evidence, both scientific and textual that Mars once hosted flowing rivers, lakes, and perhaps even a habitable environment. Ancient astronaut theorists, notably Zecharia Sitchin, took this a step further. In his writings, he proposed that the Igigi, a group of divine beings from Sumerian texts, once maintained an outpost on Mars, whom he called Lamu (others render it Lacmu).

According to Sitchin, and the Moorehens a catastrophic storm rendered Mars uninhabitable, forcing the Igigi to remain on Earth permanently. This, he argued, could explain why orbital photographs have revealed anomalous structures on the Martian surface: they were built by the Igigi during their time there.

But who were the Igigi?

Sumerian and Akkadian sources consistently identify them as the younger generation of deities, the sons of God. Consider this hymn to Marduk, preserved in cuneiform and translated by scholars at the University of Oxford as part of the Electronic Text Corpus of Sumerian Literature:

"King who gathers up the divine powers of heaven and earth. Foremost Son of Enki. Marduk, Mighty Lord, Perfect Hero. Foremost of the Great Princes. A name for the Igigi Gods. Strong one of the Anuna, the Great Gods who have given him justice and judgment..."

Here, Marduk, a central figure among the Igigi is explicitly called the "*Foremost Son of Enki*", placing him within a divine lineage. This supports the view that the Igigi were not primordial creators but descendants of the senior gods, particularly Enki, who is elsewhere identified as the leader of the elder Anunnaki.

This contrasts with an older interpretation by L. W. King in his 1910 translation of the Enuma Elish, where he described the Igigi as "older gods." But this appears to be a misreading. Later discoveries and more complete tablet translations clarify that the Anunnaki were the senior pantheon, while the Igigi served as their junior counterparts. It's likely that King, working with incomplete materials in the early 20th century, lacked the full textual context now available.

Modern scholarship affirms this distinction. As noted in academic summaries of Mesopotamian religion, "*the Igigi are generally considered to be younger gods or deities… The term Igigi itself is believed to derive from the Sumerian word I.G.I., meaning 'youth' or 'youthful ones.'*"

Further evidence comes from The Babylonian Legends of the Creation, published by the British Museum, which references:

"*The primitive gods Lacmu and Lacamu and the Igigi… who may be regarded as star gods…*"

Crucially, the same text describes how divine stations were assigned:

"*He hath allotted stations to the Igigi and the Anunnaki.*"

This aligns with Sitchin's interpretation: the Igigi were given a specific celestial post, possibly Mars as an observation or mining outpost. In The 12th Planet, Sitchin quotes a reconstructed passage he attributes to ancient records:

"Those who on earth are shall as Anunnaki be known, those who from heaven to earth came. Those who on Lamu are, Igigi shall be named, those who observe and see they shall be."

Thus, the Igigi were not abstract spirits but physical, stationed beings, the "watchers" of the heavens.

Now consider Genesis 6, a passage long debated but rarely connected to Mesopotamian sources in mainstream theology. Yet read carefully:

"And it came to pass, when men began to multiply on the face of the earth, and daughters were born unto them, that the sons of God saw the daughters of men that they were fair; and they took them wives of all which they chose."

If the "sons of God" are the Igigi, as the Sumerian texts imply, then this is not metaphor, but memory: divine beings descended, took human women, and fathered children.

The biblical narrative continues with a striking admission:

"And the Lord said, My spirit shall not always strive with man, for that he also is flesh."

Note the phrase: *"he also is flesh."* This is not poetic language, it is a direct acknowledgment that the *"sons of God"* were physical, mortal in form, just as humans are. There is no theological loophole here; the text states plainly that these beings possessed fleshly bodies.

It goes further:

"There were giants in the earth in those days; and also after that, when the sons of God came in unto the daughters of men, and they bare children to them, the same became mighty men, which were of old, men of renown."

These "giants", the Nephilim were the hybrid offspring of divine and human unions. If the Anunnaki (and their junior kin, the Igigi) stood 8 to 12 feet tall (if not taller), as Sitchin and ancient depictions suggest, then such offspring would indeed appear as "mighty men" compared to ordinary humans of 5 to 6 feet.

Thus, Genesis 6 does not describe ethereal angels, but physical sons of God, the Igigi, who walked among us, intermarried with humanity, and left a genetic legacy recorded in both Mesopotamian tablets and the Hebrew Bible.

And the most telling line remains:

"My spirit shall not always strive with man, for that he also is flesh."

A sentence so plain, so direct, that it dismantles centuries of allegorical reinterpretation.

The *"sons of God"* were flesh, because they were beings like us, yet greater: the younger gods, the Igigi, the stationed watchers from the heavens.

Remember their name. They were not myth. They were the sons of God.

Chapter 18

Important tablets

Here are some direct translations of tablets, you might find them interesting:

Kumarbi was a major deity in **Hurrian mythology**, a Bronze Age culture centered in what is now eastern Anatolia (modern-day Turkey) and northern Mesopotamia. He played a central role in the **Kumarbi Cycle**, a series of mythological texts that describe the struggle for divine kingship among the gods—particularly between Kumarbi and his son, the storm god **Teshub** (also called Tarhunna in Hittite sources).

Kingship of heaven

The *""Kingship in Heaven"1"* (from the Hittite Theogony) draws on Mesopotamian traditions of divine succession and cosmic order, often paralleling Sumerian and Babylonian myths where the Anunnaki, a collective of major deities descended from An (heaven) and Ki (earth), play central roles.

These gods are depicted in heavenly assemblies (e.g., Upšukkinaku, the *""place of decrees"1"*), as creators or overseers of humanity (to relieve divine labor), and as patrons of monumental building projects like temples and ziggurats, which symbolized the link between heaven and earth.

Let the mighty gods hearken, let Nara, Napsara, Minki, Ammunki hearken, let Ammezzaddu, father and mother, hearken! Let Ishara, father and mother, hearken! Let Enlil, who are mighty gods, and Kululimma hearken!

Formerly, in former years, Alalu was king in heaven. Alalu was sitting on the throne, and the mighty Anu, the first of the gods, was standing in front of him. He bowed down to his feet and placed the cups for drinking into his hand.

Nine full years Alalu was king in heaven. In the ninth year, Anu fought against Alalu; he overcame Alalu, so that he fled from him and went down to the dark earth. He went down to the dark earth, while Anu sat on his throne.

Anu was sitting on the throne, and the mighty Kumarbi was giving him to drink. He bowed down to his feet and placed the cups for drinking into his hands.

Nine full years Anu was king in heaven. In the ninth year, Anu fought against Kumarbi. Kumarbi, in the place of Alalu, fought against Anu. Anu could not withstand Kumarbi's eyes any more; he escaped from Kumarbi's hand and fled. Anu, as a bird, flew toward heaven.

After him Kumarbi rushed and took Anu by the feet and pulled him down from heaven. He bit his knees, so that his manhood was absorbed into Kumarbi's interior like... When Kumarbi had swallowed Anu's manhood, he rejoiced and laughed.

Anu turned back to him and spoke to Kumarbi:

"You feel joy about your interior because you have swallowed my manhood. Do not feel joy about your interior! Into your interior I have laid a seed: first I have impregnated you with the heavy Weather-God; secondly I have impregnated you with the river Aranzah; thirdly I have impregnated you with the heavy god Talmišu. Three fearful gods I have laid as a seed into your interior. In the end you shall have to strike the rocks of the mountains with your head!"

When Anu had finished his speech, he went up to heaven. Thereupon he hid. Out of his mouth he spat—Kumarbi, the wise king. Out of his mouth he spat... mixed. What Kumarbi had spat...

The angry Kumarbi went into Nippur... He sat. Kumarbi did not... He counts. Seven (or perhaps nine) months passed...

The Song of the Hoe

""The Song of the Hoe"1" (also known as ""Enki and the World Order"1") is a major Sumerian creation myth and hymn that praises the god Enki. It is absolutely central to the argument in your book, and it's easy to see why.

The poem celebrates the god Enki as the master organizer and civilizing force of the world. Key events include:

1.Creation of the Universe: It describes a primordial time when heaven and earth were separated. The supreme god, Enlil, separates the heavens (An) from the earth (Ki).

2. The Miraculous Hoe: This is the most famous part. To help humans begin the work of civilization, Enki uses his *""hoe"1"* – a divine, magical tool – to break the hard crust of the earth. From the hole he creates, humanity itself springs forth from the earth like a plant.

3. Establishing Civilization (The *""ME"1"*): Enki then *""decrees the fates"1"* and organizes the world. He assigns roles and invents the fundamental aspects of civilization (called the *""ME"1"* in Sumerian).

This includes:

- Establishing kingship and priesthood.
- Creating and assigning all arts, crafts, and technologies: agriculture, writing, metalworking, building, etc.
- Defining the characteristics of cities and lands.

4. Enki's Journey: The god travels throughout Sumer, visiting major cities like Eridu, Ur, and Meluhha, blessing them and establishing their specific cultural identities and economic specialties.

The Song of the Hoe (Enki's Praise)

This is a Sumerian hymn (ETCSL 5.5.4, ca. 2100 BCE) praising Enlil's invention of the hoe (al) as a tool of creation, agriculture, and civilization. The text plays on the syllable al (hoe) throughout, using wordplay with related terms. Below is the full English translation from the Electronic Text Corpus of Sumerian Literature (ETCSL), structured by line groups as in the original. I've included the introductory note for context.

Introductory Context from ETCSL:

In this composition, the word al 'hoe' is used as often as possible, as well as many nouns or verb forms beginning with -- or merely containing -- the syllable al (occasionally also ar).

Not only did the lord make the world appear in its correct form -- the lord who never changes the destinies which he determines: Enlil, who will make the human seed of the Land come forth (3 mss. have instead: up) from the earth (2 other mss. have instead: chamber) -- and not only did he hasten to separate heaven from earth, and hasten to separate earth from heaven, but, in order to make it possible for humans to grow in 'Where Flesh Came Forth' (2 mss. have instead: 'Where Flesh Grew') [the name of a cosmic location], he first suspended (2 mss. have instead: raised) the axis of the world at Dur-an-ki.

He did this with the help of the hoe (al) -- and so daylight broke forth (aled). By distributing (altare) the shares of duty he established daily tasks, and for the hoe (al) and the carrying-basket wages were even established. Then Enlil praised his hoe (al), his hoe (al) wrought in gold, its top inlaid with lapis lazuli, his hoe (al) whose blade was tied on with a cord, which was adorned with silver and gold, his hoe (al), the edge of whose point (?) was a plough of lapis lazuli, whose blade was like a battering ram standing up to a great (gal) wall (1 ms. has instead: born for a great (gal) person (?)). The lord evaluated the hoe (al), determined its future destiny and placed a holy crown on its head.......

[18-27]

Here, in 'Where Flesh Came Forth' (1 ms. has instead: 'Where Flesh Grew') [the name of a cosmic location], he set this very hoe (al) to work; (1 other ms. has instead: in 'Where Flesh Grew' the unassailable (?),) he had it place the first model of mankind in the brick mould. His Land started to break through the soil towards Enlil. He looked with favour at his black-headed people. Now the Anuna gods stepped forward to him, and did (jal) obeisance to him. They calmed Enlil with a prayer, for they wanted to demand (al-dug) the black-headed people from him. Ninmena, the lady who had given birth to the ruler, who had given birth to the king, now set (aljaja) human reproduction going.

[28-34]
The leader of heaven and earth, lord Nunamnir, named the important persons and valued (kal) persons. He...... these persons, and recruited them to provide for the gods. Now Enki praised Enlil's hoe (al), and the maiden Nisaba was made responsible for keeping records of the decisions. And so people took (jal) the shining hoes (al), the holy hoes (al), into their hands.

[35-42]
The E-kur, the temple of Enlil, was founded by the hoe (al). By day it was building (aldue) it, by night it caused the temple to grow (almumu). In well-founded Nibru, the hero Ninurta entered into the presence of Enlil in the inner chamber of the Tummal -- the Tummal, the bread basket (?) (1 ms. has instead:...... masterpiece (?)) of mother Ninlil -- the innermost chamber of the Tummal, with regular food deliveries. Holy Ninisina entered into the presence of Enlil with black kids and fruit offerings for the lord.

[43-45]

Next comes the Abzu, with the lions before it, where the divine powers may not be requested (al-dug): the hoe wielder (?) (altar), the good man, lord Nudimmud was building (aldue) the Abzu, Eridug having been chosen as the construction site (altar).

[46-48]
The mother of the gods, Ninhursaja, had the mighty (?) (altar) light of the lord live with her in Kec; she had Cul-pa-eda, no less, help her with the construction work (altar).

[49-51]
The shrine E-ana was cleaned up by means of the hoe (al) for the lady of E-ana, the good cow (immal) (2 mss. have instead: woman). The hoe (al) deals with ruin mounds, the hoe (al) deals with weeds.

[52-55]
In the city of Zabalam, the hoe (al) is Inana's workman (?). She determined the destiny of the hoe (al), with its projecting lapis-lazuli beard (1 ms. has instead: tooth). Utu was ready to help her with her building project (altar); it is the renowned (?) building project (altar) of youthful Utu.

[56-58]
The lady with broad (dajal) intelligence, Nisaba, ordered the measuring of the E-ana for a construction project (altar), and then designed her own E-hamun for construction (altar).

[59-70]

The king who measured up the hoe (*al*) and who passes (*zal*) his time in its tracks, the hero Ninurta, has introduced working with the hoe (*altar*) into the rebel (*bal*) lands. He subdues (*aljaja*) any city that does not obey its lord. Towards heaven he roars (*algigi*) like a storm, earthwards he strikes (*aljaja*) like a dragon (*ucumgal*). Cara sat down on (1 ms. has instead: got onto) Enlil's knees, and Enlil gave him what he had desired (*al-dug*): he had mentioned the mace, the club, arrows and quiver, and the hoe (*al*) (3 mss. have instead: he desired (*al-dug*) the mace, the club, arrows and quiver). Dumuzid is the one who makes the upper land fertile (*allumlum*). Gibil made his hoe (*al*) raise its head towards the heavens -- he caused the hoe (*al*), sacred indeed, to be refined with fire. The Anuna were rejoicing (*alhulhuledec*).

[71-82]
The temple of Jectin-ana resembled an *aljarsur* instrument, the *aljarsur* of mother Jectin-ana that makes a pleasant sound. The lord [Enlil] bellowed at his hoe (*al*) like a bull. As for the grave (*irigal*): the hoe (*al*) buries people, but dead people are also brought up from the ground by the hoe (*al*) [This may allude to Enkidu's ghost being put in contact with Gilgamec.]. With the hoe (*al*), the hero honoured by An, the younger brother of Nergal, the warrior Gilgamec is as powerful as a hunting net. The (1 ms. adds: sage) son of Ninsumun is pre-eminent with oars (*jisal*) [This may allude to Gilgamec rowing across the waters of death.]. With the hoe (*al*) he is the great barber (*kindajal*) of the watercourses. In the chamber (1 ms. has instead: place) of the shrine, with the hoe (*al*) he is the minister (*sukkal*). The wicked (*huljal*)...... are sons of the hoe (*al*); they are born in sleep from heaven.

[83-93]

In the sky there is the altirigu bird, the bird of the god. On the earth there is the hoe (al): a dog in the reed-beds, a dragon (ucumgal) in the forest. On the battlefield, there is the dur-allub battle-axe. By the city wall there is the battle-net (alluhab). On the dining-table there is the bowl (maltum). In the waggon shed, there is the sledge (mayaltum). In the donkey stable there is the cupboard (argibil). The hoe (al)! -- the sound of the word is sweet: it also occurs (munjal) on the hillsides: the tree of the hillsides is the allanum oak. The fragrance of the hillsides is the arganum balm. The precious stone of the hillsides is the algamec steatite.

[94-106]
The hoe (al) makes everything prosper, the hoe makes everything flourish. The hoe (al) is good barley, the hoe (al) is a hunting net (1 ms. has instead: an overseer). The hoe (al) is brick moulds, the hoe (al) has made people exist (jal). It is the hoe (al) that is the strength of young manhood. The hoe (al) and the basket are the tools for building cities. It builds (aldue) the right kind of house, it cultivates (aljaja) the right kind of fields. It is you, hoe, that extend (dajal) the good agricultural land! The hoe (al) subdues for its owner (lugal) any agricultural lands that have been recalcitrant (bal) against their owner (lugal), any agricultural lands that have not submitted to their owner (lugal). It chops the heads off the vile esparto grasses, yanks them out at their roots, and tears at their stalks. The hoe (al) also subdues (aljaja) the hirin weeds.

[107-109]
The hoe (al), the implement whose destiny was fixed by father Enlil -- the renowned hoe (al)! Nisaba be praised!

The cursing of Agade: translation

THE CURSING OF AGADE (also known as *THE CURSE OF AKKAD*) is an ancient Sumerian literary text, likely composed several centuries after the fall of the Akkadian Empire (circa 2334–2154 BCE). It recounts the rise and catastrophic collapse of the city of Akkad (Agade), the capital founded by Sargon of Akkad.

The narrative attributes the empire's downfall to divine punishment—specifically, the wrath of the god Enlil—triggered by King Naram-Sin's (Sargon's grandson) alleged act of desecrating Enlil's temple in Nippur. According to the text, Naram-Sin, frustrated by silence from the gods, plundered the Ekur temple, which enraged Enlil. In response, Enlil summoned the Gutians,(See my video called real planet of the apes) a mountain people described as uncivilized and barbaric, to invade Mesopotamia and bring chaos.

The poem vividly describes the resulting societal collapse: famine, economic ruin, abandonment of cities, and the breakdown of order. Akkad is ultimately cursed and left desolate, with its location lost to history (archaeologists still debate where Agade was).

Old Babylonian version

1–9
After Enlil's frown had slain Kiš as if it were the Bull of Heaven, had slaughtered the house of the land of Unug in the dust as if it were a mighty bull, and then Enlil had given the rulership and kingship from the south as far as the highlands to Sargon, king of Agade—at that time, holy Inana established the sanctuary of Agade as her celebrated woman's domain; she set up her throne in Ulmaš.

10–24
Like a young man building a house for the first time, like a girl establishing a woman's domain, holy Inana did not sleep as she ensured that the warehouses would be provisioned; that dwellings would be founded in the city; that its people would eat splendid food; that its people would drink splendid beverages; that those bathed for holidays would rejoice in the courtyards; that the people would throng the places of celebration; that acquaintances would dine together; that foreigners would cruise about like unusual birds in the sky; that even Marhaši would be re-entered on the tribute rolls; that monkeys, mighty elephants, water buffalo, exotic animals, as well as thoroughbred dogs, lions, mountain ibexes (some mss. have instead: mountain beasts (?) or horses), and alum sheep with long wool would jostle each other in the public squares.

25–39
She then filled Agade's stores for emmer wheat with gold, she filled its stores for white emmer wheat with silver; she delivered copper, tin, and blocks of lapis lazuli to its granaries and sealed its silos from outside.

She endowed its old women with the gift of giving counsel, she endowed its old men with the gift of eloquence.

She endowed its young women with the gift of entertaining, she endowed its young men with martial might, she endowed its little ones with joy. The nursemaids who cared for (some mss. have instead: of) the general's children played the aljaršur instruments. Inside the city tigi drums sounded; outside it, flutes and zamzam instruments. Its harbour where ships moored was full of joy. All foreign lands rested contentedly, and their people experienced happiness.

40–56
Its king, the shepherd Naram-Suen, rose as the daylight on the holy throne of Agade. Its city wall, like a mountain (1 ms. has instead: a great mountain), reached the heavens. It was like the Tigris going to (some mss. have instead: flowing into) the sea as holy Inana opened the portals of its city-gates and made Sumer bring its own possessions upstream by boats.

The highland Martu, people ignorant of agriculture, brought spirited cattle and kids for her.

The Meluhans, the people of the black land, brought exotic wares (some mss. have instead: wares of foreign countries) up to her. Elam and Subir loaded themselves with goods for her as if they were packasses. All the governors, the temple administrators (1 ms. has instead: generals), and the accountants of the Gu-edina regularly supplied the monthly and New Year offerings. What a weariness all these caused at Agade's city gates!

Holy Inana could hardly receive all these offerings. As if she were a citizen there, she could not restrain (?) the desire (?) to prepare the ground for a temple.

57–65

But the statement coming from the E-kur was disquieting. Because of Enlil (?) all Agade was reduced (?) to trembling, and terror befell Inana in Ulmaš. She left the city, returning to her home. aHoly Inana abandoned the sanctuary of Agade like someone abandoning the young women of her woman's domain. Like a warrior hurrying to arms, she removed (some mss. have instead: tore away) the gift of battle and fight from the city and handed them over to the enemy.

66–76a

Not even five or ten days had passed and Ninurta brought the jewels of rulership, the royal crown, the emblem and the royal throne bestowed on Agade, back into his E-šumeša. Utu took away the eloquence of the city.

Enki took away its wisdom. An took up (some mss. have instead: out or away) (1 ms. has instead: away) into the midst of heaven its fearsomeness that reaches heaven. Enki tore out its well-anchored holy mooring pole from the abzu. Inana took away its weapons.

77–82

The life of Agade's sanctuary was brought to an end as if it had been only the life of a tiny carp in the deep waters, and all the cities were watching it. Like a mighty elephant, it bent its neck to the ground while they all raised their horns like mighty bulls. Like a dying dragon, it dragged its head on the earth and they jointly deprived it of honour as in a battle.

83–93

Naram-Suen saw in a nocturnal vision that Enlil would not let the kingdom of Agade occupy a pleasant, lasting residence, that he would make its future altogether unfavourable, that he would make its temples shake and would scatter its treasures .

He realized what the dream was about, but did not put into words, and did not discuss it with anyone. (1 ms. adds 2 lines: ...... temples shake......, ... perform (?) extispicy regarding (?) his temple......) Because of the E-kur, he put on mourning clothes, covered his chariot with a reed mat (1 ms. has instead: pulled out the outside pin of his chariot), tore the reed canopy off his ceremonial barge (1 ms. has instead: the prow of his ceremonial barge or the cabin of his ceremonial barge), and gave away his royal paraphernalia.

Naram-Suen persisted for seven years! Who has ever seen a king burying his head in his hands for seven years? (some mss. add the line: He realized what the dream was about, but did not put into words, and did not discuss it with anyone.)

94–99
Then he went to perform extispicy on a kid regarding the temple, but the omen had nothing to say about the building of the temple. For a second time he went to perform extispicy on a kid regarding the temple, but the omen again had nothing to say about the building of the temple. In order to change what had been inflicted (?) upon him, he tried to alter Enlil's pronouncement.

100–119
Because his subjects were dispersed, he now began a mobilization of his troops. Like a wrestler who is about to enter the great courtyard, he...... his hands towards (?) the E-kur. Like an athlete bent to start a contest, he treated the giguna as if it were worth only thirty shekels.

Like a robber plundering the city, he set tall ladders against the temple.

To demolish E-kur as if it were a huge ship, to break up its soil like the soil of mountains where precious metals are mined, to splinter it like the lapis lazuli mountain, to prostrate it, like a city inundated by Ickur.

Though the temple was not a mountain where cedars are felled, he had large axes cast, he had double-edged agasilig axes sharpened to be used against it. He set spades against its roots and it sank as low as the foundation of the Land. He put axes against its top, and the temple, like a dead soldier, bowed its neck before him, and all the foreign lands bowed their necks before him.

120–148
He ripped out its drain pipes, and all the rain went back to the heavens. He tore off its upper lintel and the Land was deprived of its ornament (1 ms. has instead: the ornament of the Land disappeared). From its "Gate from which grain is never diverted," he diverted grain, and the Land was deprived of grain. He struck the "Gate of Well-Being" with the pickaxe, and well-being was subverted in all the foreign lands.

As if they were for great tracts of land with wide carp-filled waters, he cast large spades (1 ms. has instead: axes) to be used against the E-kur. The people could see the bedchamber, its room which knows no daylight.

The Akkadians could look into the holy treasure chest of the gods. Though they had committed no sacrilege, its lahama deities of the great pilasters standing at the temple were thrown into the fire by Naram-Suen.

The cedar, cypress, juniper and boxwood, the woods of its giguna, were...... by him. He put its gold in containers and put its silver in leather bags.

He filled the docks with its copper, as if it were a huge transport of grain. The silversmiths were re-shaping its silver, jewellers were re-shaping its precious stones, smiths were beating its copper.

Large ships were moored at the temple, large ships were moored at Enlil's temple and its possessions were taken away from the city, though they were not the goods of a plundered city. With the possessions being taken away from the city, good sense left Agade. As the ships moved away from (some mss. have instead: juddered) the docks, Agade's intelligence (1 ms. has instead: sanctuary) was removed.

149–175
Enlil, the roaring (?) storm that subjugates the entire land, the rising deluge that cannot be confronted, was considering what should be destroyed in return for the wrecking of his beloved E-kur. He lifted his gaze towards the Gubin mountains, and made all the inhabitants of the broad mountain ranges descend (?). Enlil brought out of the mountains those who do not resemble other people, who are not reckoned as part of the Land, the Gutians, an unbridled people, with human intelligence but canine instincts (some mss. have instead: feelings) and monkeys' features.

Like small birds they swooped on the ground in great flocks. Because of Enlil, they stretched their arms out across the plain like a net for animals. Nothing escaped their clutches, no one left their grasp. Messengers no longer travelled the highways, the courier's boat no longer passed along the rivers. The Gutians drove the trusty (?) goats of Enlil out of their folds and compelled their herdsmen to follow them, they drove the cows out of their pens and compelled their cowherds to follow them.

Prisoners manned the watch. Brigands occupied (1 ms. has instead: attacked) the highways. The doors of the city gates of the Land lay dislodged in (1 ms. has instead: were covered with) mud, and all the foreign lands uttered bitter cries from the walls of their cities.

They established gardens for themselves (1 ms. has instead: made gardens grow) within the cities, and not as usual on the wide plain outside. As if it had been before the time when cities were built and founded, the large (some mss. add: fields and) arable tracts yielded no grain, the inundated (some mss. add: fields and) tracts yielded no fish, the irrigated orchards yielded no syrup or wine, the thick clouds (?) did not rain, the mašgurum plant did not grow.

176–192

In those days, oil for one shekel was only half a litre, grain for one shekel was only half a litre, wool for one shekel was only one mina, fish for one shekel filled only one ban measure—these sold at such prices in the markets of the cities! Those who lay down on the roof, died on the roof; those who lay down in the house were not buried.

People were flailing at themselves from hunger. By the Ki-ur, Enlil's great place, dogs were packed together in the silent streets; if two men walked there they would be devoured by them, and if three men walked there they would be devoured by them. Noses were punched (?), heads were smashed (?), noses (?) were piled up, heads were sown like seeds.

Honest people were confounded with traitors, heroes lay dead on top of heroes, the blood of traitors ran upon the blood of honest men.

193–209

At that time, Enlil rebuilt his great sanctuaries into small reed (?) sanctuaries and from east to west he reduced their storehouses.

The old women who survived those days, the old men who survived those days and the chief lamentation singer who survived those years set up seven balaj drums, as if they stood at the horizon, and together with ub, meze, and lilis (some mss. have instead: cem, and lilis) (1 ms. has instead: and bronze cem) drums made them resound to Enlil like Ickur for seven days and seven nights.

The old women did not restrain the cry "Alas for my city!" The old men did not restrain the cry "Alas for its people!" The lamentation singer did not restrain the cry "Alas for the E-kur!" Its young women did not restrain from tearing their hair. Its young men did not restrain from sharpening their knives.

Their laments were as if Enlil's ancestors were performing a lament in the awe-inspiring Holy Mound by the holy knees of Enlil. Because of this, Enlil entered his holy bedchamber and lay down fasting.

210–221

At that time, Suen, Enki, Inana, Ninurta, Ickur, Utu, Nuska, and Nisaba, the great gods (1 ms. has instead: all the gods whosoever), cooled (1 ms. has instead: sprinkled) Enlil's heart with cool water and prayed to him: "Enlil, may the city that destroyed your city, be treated as your city has been treated!

May the one that defiled your giguna, be treated as Nibru! In this city, may heads fill the wells! May no one find his acquaintances there, may brother not recognize brother! May its young woman be cruelly killed in her woman's domain, may its old man cry in distress for his slain wife! May its pigeons moan on their window ledges, may its small birds be smitten in their nooks, may it live in constant anxiety like a timid pigeon!"

222–244

Again, Suen, Enki, Inana, Ninurta, Ickur, Utu, Nuska, and Nisaba, all the gods whosoever, turned their attention to the city, and cursed Agade severely:

"City, you pounced on E-kur: it is as if you had pounced on Enlil!
Agade, you pounced on E-kur: it is as if you had pounced on Enlil!
May your holy walls, to their highest point, resound with mourning!
May your giguna be reduced to a pile of dust!
May your pilasters with the standing lahama deities fall to the ground like tall young men drunk on wine!
May your clay be returned to its abzu, may it be clay cursed by Enki!

May your grain be returned to its furrow, may it be grain cursed by Ezinu!
May your timber be returned to its forest, may it be timber cursed by Ninilduma!
May the (1 ms. has instead: your) cattle slaughterer slaughter his wife,
may your (some mss. have instead: the) sheep butcher butcher his child!

May water wash away your pauper as he is looking for......!
May your prostitute hang herself at the entrance to her brothel!
May your pregnant (?) hierodules and cult prostitutes abort (?) their children!
May your gold be bought for the price of silver,
may your silver be bought for the price of pyrite (?),
and may your copper be bought for the price of lead!"

245–255

"Agade, may your strong man be deprived of his strength,
so that he will be unable to lift his sack of provisions and......, and will not have the joy of controlling your superior asses; may he lie idle all day!
May this make the city die of hunger!
May your citizens, who used to eat fine food, lie hungry in the grass and herbs,
may your...... man eat the coating on his roof,
may he chew (?) the leather hinges on the main door of his father's house!
May depression descend upon your palace, built for joy (1 ms. has instead: joyous palace)!
May the evils of the desert, the silent place, howl continuously!"

256–271

"May foxes that frequent ruin mounds brush with their tails your fattening-pens (?), established for purification ceremonies!

May the ukuku, the bird of depression, make its nest in your gateways, established for the Land!
In your city that could not sleep because of the tigi drums, that could not rest from its joy,
may the bulls of Nanna that fill the pens bellow like those who wander in the desert, the silent place!

May the grass grow long on your canal-bank tow-paths, may the grass of mourning grow on your highways laid for waggons!
Moreover, may...... wild rams (?) and alert snakes of the mountains allow no one to pass on your tow-paths built up with canal sediment!

In your plains where fine grass grows, may the reed of lamentation grow!
Agade, may brackish water flow (1 ms. has instead: May brackish water flow in the river), where fresh water flowed for you!

If someone decides, 'I will dwell in this city!', may he not enjoy the pleasures of a dwelling place!
If someone decides, 'I will rest in Agade!', may he not enjoy the pleasures of a resting place!"

272–280
And before Utu on that very day, so it was!
On its canal bank tow-paths, the grass grew long.
On its highways laid for waggons, the grass of mourning grew.

Moreover, on its tow-paths built up with canal sediment, ...

wild rams (?) and alert snakes of the mountains allowed no one to pass.

On its plains, where fine grass grew, now the reeds of lamentation grew.
Agade's flowing fresh water flowed as brackish water.
When someone decided, "I will dwell in that city!", he could not enjoy the pleasures of a dwelling place.
When someone decided, "I will rest in Agade!", he could not enjoy the pleasures of a resting place!

281
Inana be praised for the destruction of Agade!

Chapter 19

Almighty God

Strange things an Almighty being does in the bible that really feels like it should be for a living person.

The Bible often describes God using human-like traits (anthropomorphisms) or actions that suggest limitations, emotions, or dependencies inconsistent with an absolutely omnipotent, omniscient, and unchanging being. These can include physical actions, emotional responses, regrets, or needs for information/intervention. Below is a curated list of examples, drawn from key passages. Note that interpretations vary, some see these as metaphorical accommodations for human understanding, while others view them as textual tensions. I've included the user's examples where applicable and expanded with similar instances for completeness.

Regrets creating humanity, then relies on Noah for preservation **(Genesis 6:5-8):** God "regrets" making humans, grieves in His heart, and decides to wipe out all life with a flood, yet instructs Noah to build an ark to save a remnant, implying a need for human cooperation to avert total self-contradiction.

Commands elaborate bread offerings ("cakes") for Himself via Moses (Leviticus 24:5-9; Exodus 25:30): God directs the Israelites to bake twelve "cakes" of fine flour (showbread) weekly and place them before Him in the tabernacle as a perpetual offering, suggesting a desire for ritual sustenance, like a divine snack service managed by humans.

"Rests" after creation, implying fatigue (Genesis 2:2-3): On the seventh day, God "rests from all his work," which the commandment in Exodus 20:11 explicitly models human Sabbath rest upon, portraying divine exhaustion after labor.

Searches for and questions Adam and Eve's location (Genesis 3:8-9): After they hide, God "walks" in the garden and calls out, "Where are you?", as if unaware of their position despite being the all-seeing Creator.

Inquires about Abel's whereabouts after Cain's murder (Genesis 4:9-10): God asks Cain, "Where is your brother Abel?", appearing to lack foreknowledge of the crime He confronts.

Descends to investigate Sodom personally (Genesis 18:20-21): Despite reports of outcry reaching Him, God says, "I will go down and see if what they have done deserves destruction", suggesting a need for firsthand verification rather than omniscience.

Smells the aroma of Noah's sacrifice and is "pleased" (Genesis 8:21): After the flood, God inhales the burnt offering and vows never to curse the ground again—depicting olfactory pleasure influencing a change of heart.

Tests Abraham's faith without prior knowledge of the outcome (Genesis 22:1-12): God commands the sacrifice of Isaac, then stops it, saying, "Now I know that you fear God", implying He learned something new through the trial.

Repents (changes mind) multiple times due to human pleas: Examples include relenting on destroying Israel after the golden calf (Exodus 32:14), sparing Nineveh after Jonah's preaching (Jonah 3:10), and regretting making Saul king (1 Samuel 15:11, 35), contradicting immutability (Malachi 3:6).

Wrestles physically with Jacob and appears to tire/injure (Genesis 32:24-30): A "man" (identified as God) grapples with Jacob all night, has his hip touched to dislocate it, and demands a blessing, portraying a corporeal struggle with limits.

Comes down to confuse languages at Babel due to human ambition (Genesis 11:5-7): God "comes down" to see the tower, then scatters people, as if the threat required direct intervention rather than effortless prevention.

Feels "sorry" and is "grieved" over human wickedness (Genesis 6:6): Echoing the flood regret, this emotional turmoil precedes the deluge, humanizing God with sorrow like a disappointed parent.

Experiences jealousy and anger like a possessive spouse (Exodus 20:5; 34:14): God describes Himself as a "jealous God" who visits iniquity on generations, attributing human emotions of rivalry and wrath.

Shows pity or compassion in response to cries (Judges 2:18): God "could bear it no longer" and raises deliverers, suggesting emotional limits where human suffering moves Him to act, rather than proactive omnipotence.

Sits on a throne in numerous visionary depictions (e.g., Isaiah 6:1; Ezekiel 1:26; Daniel 7:9; Psalm 47:8; Revelation 4:2): God is portrayed "sitting" enthroned at least a dozen times across prophetic visions (with echoes in Psalms and elsewhere potentially reaching 20+ if including "dwells" or "abides" variants), implying a seated, localized posture rather than boundless transcendence.

Uses physical body parts in actions: God has "hands" (Exodus 15:17, to plant Israel), "arms" stretched out (Exodus 6:6, in deliverance), "eyes" that see (Genesis 6:8, favoring Noah), a "mouth" that speaks (Numbers 12:8), "nostrils" that flare (Exodus 15:8, in wind), and even "wings" and "feathers" for shelter (Psalm 91:4), all evoking a humanoid form.

Limits miracles based on human unbelief (Mark 6:5-6): Jesus (as God incarnate) "could not do any miracles there, except lay his hands on a few sick people," and "was amazed at their lack of faith", indicating divine power constrained by human response.

Hope you enjoyed this book.
Please remember there is also book 1 of this book.

I do have a website with documentaries, live chats, maps, Anunnaki family tree and much more.

Here's just some of the documentaries I have on my site:

www.ourtruehistory.co.uk

- Giants Were Real!
- Ultimate Elongated Skull Video
- Atlantis
- Everything You Need to Know About Mermaids
- Everything About Aliens
- UFOs: How They Fly!
- Debunking the Debunkers! Aliens, Anunnaki, Fake Stuff
- Stonehenge
- Crash Course on the Anunnaki - Extended Version
- Anunnaki Family Tree (Interactive)
- Enuma Elish Tablets (Full Series, Read by OTH)
- Norse Gods Series
- The Great Flood - All You Need to Know
- Time Travel
- Bigfoot
- Crystal Skulls
- **And so much more!**

Printed in Dunstable, United Kingdom